Conte

D0625535

FIGURES

TABLES

Acknowledgements

It is with pleasure that I acknowledge my indebtedness to the following for their help during the research and writing of this study:

To Professor R.V. Comerford, Dr Colm Lennon and the teaching staff of the Department of Modern History, NUI, Maynooth. To Dr Jacinta Prunty and Dr Raymond Gillespie for their invaluable inspiration, guidance and assistance. To the staff of the following institutions who were always helpful and courteous: John Paul II Library, NUI, Maynooth; National Library of Ireland; National Archives; Dublin Diocesan Archives; Irish Church Missions Archives; Irish Architectural Archives; Representative Church Body Library. To family members for their encouragement. I acknowledge the help, advice and fellowship of my colleagues in the 1998-2000 NUI, Maynooth MA in Local History class. For Dan Moloney, my guiding light.

Introduction

The archdiocese of Tuam covers a vast geographical area in Counties Galway and Mayo. It is almost bisected by Loughs Corrib, Mask and Carra. The eastern portion is limestone plain containing the finest land in Connacht, but also some bogs which are drained into the lakes by the rivers Clare and Robe. West of the lakes there is mountain, heather and rock with some fertile valleys enclosed by the sheltering hills. Two hundred years ago, the most western part of it was one of the most over-populated and under-developed parts of Ireland and relatively inaccessible except by venturing along the Atlantic coastline indented by numerous bays and inlets. In the 1820s a road-building scheme was undertaken. This opened up vast tracts of land in west Mayo and to the west and north west of Galway city. These tracts were to a great extent rough mountainous, inhospitable country suitable only for raising sheep. The archdiocese contained 39 per cent of County Galway and 57 per cent of County Mayo with a small portion of County Roscommon, in all, 1,388,290 statute acres for, in 1834, a population of 378,021 persons.[1]

From the 1780s the British government tried to address the elementary education of the poor people of Ireland. It was accused of sectarianism, which was an issue inextricably entwined with state schools. This was a policy established in the time of Elizabeth I, when it was realised that the setting up of parish schools was essential for the spread of Protestantism and of the English language. Financing was entrusted to the clergy of the Established Church – who were supported by tithes – collected from all the landholders in the diocese although the population was, in 1834, 97 per cent Roman Catholic.[2] Under the penal laws, Roman Catholics were forbidden to be schoolteachers; from 1782, they were permitted to teach school under licence from the Protestant bishop of the diocese. In 1787 the chain of events, which over the next half a century would produce the national schools system, began with a plan to reactivate the parish schools, introduced by Thomas Orde[3] in the Irish parliament. He envisaged twenty-two diocesan schools that would lay the foundations in classical learning. Funding from a local rate on wealthy proprietors would augment the Protestant clerical funding. A special fund to be known as the lord lieutenant's school fund would be applied to purchase and build schools to provide free elementary education to the poor of all denominations. Much to the dismay of Catholics, the plan envisaged that those benefiting from the school system should be brought up in the Protestant religion. The same ideas had been tried and abandoned in Charter

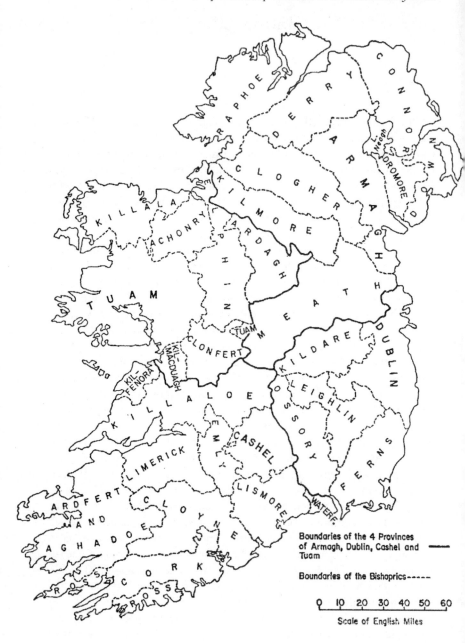

Boundaries of the 4 Provinces
of Armagh, Dublin, Cashel and ⎯⎯⎯
Tuam

Boundaries of the Bishoprics ⎯⎯⎯⎯

0   10   20   30   40   50   60

Scale of English Miles

1. The provinces and dioceses of Ireland

Schools nearly forty years earlier. The bishops were aghast at what they perceived as regression in Orde's proposals. In February 1788, Boetius Egan, Roman Catholic archbishop of Tuam, regarded them as hostile to the interests of the Catholic religion and as a way of increasing the British and Protestant stranglehold on the Catholics of Ireland. Orde's plan, though never implemented, opened up a debate on the provision of education for the masses. Then in 1791 a significant convergence of opinion between both religions occurred, when a commission of inquiry into the funding of schools recommended the novel idea that Roman Catholic and Protestant pupils would be educated together for literary instruction and separately for religious instruction. This report, though never presented to parliament, was eventually published in 1857.

In 1806 another inquiry was instituted. John Leslie Foster, baron of the exchequer and a kinsman of the future Lady Plunket wife of Thomas Plunket, Protestant bishop of Tuam was a commissioner of education. That commission produced fourteen reports between 1809 and 1821. Their thirteenth report greatly influenced Irish educational practice during the nineteenth century. They recommended a permanent body of commissioners and massive state intervention in education. They were to administer parliamentary grants, using them to build new schools where necessary. In line with the proposal of 1791, in a very significant and welcome departure, it was recommended that there would be absolutely no attempt made to influence or disturb the peculiar religious tenets of any sect or description of Christian. They were to have control over all schoolbooks in their schools and they were to draw up selections of extracts from the scriptures containing religious and moral instruction. Gradually the master plan from which the national schools system for the education of the masses would materialise was designed.

The appointment, in 1812, of Sir Robert Peel as Chief Secretary for Ireland led in 1815 to a state grant for elementary education to the Society for the Education of the Poor in Ireland – usually known as the Kildare Place Society. It was established as a non-denominational body – supported by both Protestants and Roman Catholics – which maintained schools throughout the country. It trained about 280 schoolmasters and mistresses each year.[4] Oliver Kelly, Roman Catholic archbishop of Tuam, was very aware of the need for teacher training. He expressed his concern, to Thomas Franklin Lewis, chairman of the Commissioners of Irish Education, on 17 December 1825, that no provision was made in the proposed national schools regulations 'for training schools and model schools, where we can send Catholics to be educated and we should have a model school not liable to the objections that the Kildare Place Society is'.[5] The Society initially tried to be impartial in matters of religion, by having 'holy scripture read without note or comment'; however, what it presented was not at all regarded as impartial by the Roman Catholic church, as the church's principles forbade any such reading. Its schools were perceived as vehicles for proselytism, especially from 1820, when in a move away from its initial aims, it gave part of its grant to Protestant proselytising societies. This angered the Roman Catholic clergy. In February 1820 Rev. John MacHale, professor in dogmatic theology at St Patrick's College at Maynooth and a native of the west of Ireland diocese of Killala, began issuing, under the pseudonym of Hierophilos, a series of letters, in the public press, warning the clergy of the insidious schemes of the Kildare Place Society. In 1823, he stated that only one Roman Catholic pupil was funded by them for every 500 Protestant pupils funded.[6] This alarmed the episcopacy and immediately led Archbishop Kelly and the other bishops to petition the government for an inquiry into the distribution of funds for Irish education. Their demand was listened to and another inquiry was under way. The brief of this commission was to research and collate evidence on the current state of education in Ireland. Its findings, issued in 1825, showed that in Tuam archdiocese there were hundreds of unlicensed, barely tolerated hedge schools, conducted by semi-literate teachers who were paid by the parents of their scholars to provide the rudiments of education. In 1824 it was reported that English was always spoken in country schools in County Galway and that the parents were anxious that these schools should teach English.[7] The benefits of English were apparent to people such as Patrick MacHale in conducting his business away from his home and to the many people who were emigrating. In an effort at further impartiality in matters of religion, the commissioners of education recommended, in 1824–5, the appointment of two teachers in every school, one Protestant and the other Roman Catholic, to superintend separately the religious education of the children. They hoped to be able to agree on a selection from the scriptures, which might be generally acquiesced in by both persuasions. This scheme was found to be impractical. In 1828 a committee of the house of commons recommended a combined religious and separate literary system of national education to be implemented by seven government-appointed commissioners of national education in Ireland. On 23 February 1832 the Chief Secretary for Ireland, Lord Stanley, offered the presidency of the Board of National Education to the duke of Leinster.[8]

The national school system was a marvellous opportunity to make a concerted attack on illiteracy. The Roman Catholic bishops

> welcomed the rule which requires that all teachers henceforth to be employed be provided, from some model school, with a certificate of their competency, that will aid us in our work of great difficulty, to wit, that of suppressing hedge schools, and placing youth under the direction of competent teachers, and of those only.[9]

The commissioners provided an environment that effectively ignored the child's inherited culture. In this they were supported by many parents who saw in schooling a preparation for a better life, which could only be found elsewhere. The commissioners envisaged the happy mingling of children from different churches, but this was at a time of intense religious controversy between Catholics, embittered by a century of penal laws, and Protestants. Throughout the next half century John MacHale, now archbishop of Tuam, was the central character in the story of education in the archdiocese, throughout an exceptionally long episcopacy, from 1834 to his death in 1881. The development, within the Roman Catholic archdiocese of Tuam, of the system of education offered by national schools greatly affected the lives of the people there in the years 1831–81.

Both later studies and contemporary documents reveal the attitudes of John MacHale, archbishop of Tuam 1835–81, towards the national schools. *The Life of John MacHale, archbishop of Tuam* is a biography based on MacHale's manuscripts and immense correspondence which he bequeathed to his most loved and trusted nephew Thomas MacHale, rector of the Irish College, Paris. MacHale and the editor, Islandeady-man (a parish between Castlebar and Westport) Bernard O'Reilly, worked on the biography, which was published in two volumes in New York in 1890. This biography taken with *The letters (1820–1834) of the Most Rev Dr John MacHale* (Dublin, 1893) give an insight into the mind of the archbishop. Other studies, such as P.C. Barry's 'The Holy See and the Irish national schools' in *Irish Ecclesiastical Record*, xcii, (1959), and Patrick J. Corish (ed.), Irish College, Rome: 'Kirby papers' in *Archivium Hibernicum*, xxx–xxxii, (1972–4) chronicle the interaction between the Irish episcopacy and Rome. Research to date therefore has relied strongly upon the perspective on the political infighting and power struggles within and between members of the hierarchy.

John MacHale was raised to the episcopacy as the question of schooling for the masses was being re-addressed. Government assistance towards education was available, albeit through a complex, expensive and highly controversial scheme. The complexities of the situation in which Archbishop MacHale and the Protestant bishops of Tuam found themselves when faced with the intransigence of the mighty power of a British government are explored. The mistrust planted by a century of penal laws blinded both sides. The families directly concerned grasped at any schools offered to them by the clergy of both major denominations, Franciscan Brothers, Presentation Sisters, Sisters of Mercy and the Church Education Society. They all bore the brunt of very great privations. Teachers formed well-motivated groups to enhance the future possibilities of both themselves and their pupils. They achieved more in the decade following the formation of the Irish National Teachers' Organisation than had been achieved in the previous half century.

Elementary education in the archdiocese of Tuam, 1831–39

The man John MacHale was formed in surroundings of relative affluence and privilege. He was shielded, somewhat, from the great poverty which surrounded him. Born in 1791 at Tubbernavine, near Crossmolina, in north Mayo he was the son of Patrick MacHale, an enterprising inn keeper, and a linen and wool merchant in a poor, Irish speaking area. The family home was the centre where news was relayed, and information on all passing events, on religious topics as well as the stirring incidents of the time, was obtained. John was educated at Lahardane hedge school, then at Castlebar classical school, and following in the footsteps of his uncle Richard MacHale, parish priest at Addergoole,[1] he studied for the priesthood. After ordination in 1814, for his home diocese of Killala, at St Patrick's College Maynooth,[2] his talents were quickly recognised and in 1820 he was appointed professor of dogmatic theology at Maynooth[3] at an annual salary of £122. He maintained strong links with his native parish. On 22 September 1822, in a rather exceptional departure from the custom that a parish priest should reside within his parish, Dr Waldron, bishop of Killala formally conferred on him the parish of Crossmolina, while he maintained his teaching post at Maynooth.[4] He was invited to Rome, in 1823, to deliver a series of reportedly very well received theological discourses which were translated into Italian by the Abbot de Lucia, apostolic nuncio at Vienna.[5] His scholarship continued with the publication, in 1828, of his book *Evidences and doctrines of the Catholic church*.[6] On 5 June 1825, months before his thirty-fourth birthday, he was consecrated bishop-elect of Maronia at Maynooth college chapel[7] by Daniel Murray, archbishop of Dublin, assisted by the archbishop of Tuam, Oliver Kelly.[8] Paul Cullen, elevated in June 1866 as the first Irish cardinal, and Catherine MacAuley, foundress of the Sisters of Mercy, were present.[9] Murray, Cullen and the Sisters of Mercy were to feature very much in the long-running MacHale story. He returned to his native diocese as coadjutor to Dr Waldron. His consecration was the beginning of well over half a century in the forefront of the Irish church. In November 1881 the *Freeman's Journal* was to write 'John, Archbishop of Tuam, breathed his last at St Jarlath's on the 7th November 1881, in the 56th year of his episcopacy, the 67th of his priesthood, and the 90th year of his age.'[10]

John MacHale's predecessor in Tuam was the energetic, charitable, Oliver Kelly who was appointed archbishop of Tuam in 1815 at the age of thirty-eight. Educated for the priesthood at the Irish College, Salamanca, he put in place

much of the foundations upon which MacHale was to build.[11] Archbishop
Boetius Egan of Tuam (1787–1798), one of the first trustees of Maynooth
College, considered the establishment of a diocesan seminary at Tuam as a
preparatory school for Maynooth. In 1800, his successor Archbishop Dillon of
Tuam appointed Oliver Kelly as first president of the new college at Tuam,
dedicated to Jarlath the patron saint of the diocese.[12] In a shrewd manoeuvre,
calculated to involve the gentry in future diocesan plans, Kelly invited fourteen
representatives of the Roman Catholic gentry of the archdiocese – the Bellews,
Blakes, Bodkins, Brownes, Egans, Ffrenchs, Kirwans, Lynchs and Martins to
join eighteen priests on the board of management of the college.[13] One of
these gentlemen, Christopher Bellew of Mount Bellew, had an ongoing
cordial relationship with Archbishop Kelly, since with his approval, Bellew
invited the Franciscan Brothers from Merchants' Quay friary in Dublin to
open a school at Mount Bellew in 1818. In 1829 the Brothers successfully
petitioned the Holy See to be placed under the jurisdiction of the archbishop
of Tuam. From Mount Bellew they expanded rapidly in the west.[14]

The leviathan task of forming a substantial infrastructure to Tuam archdiocese exhausted Kelly. A change of scene would restore his vigour and
enthusiasm after a score years at the helm of a difficult, cash-starved ministry.
He undertook the hazardous journey to Rome shortly after Christmas 1833
and died there on 18 April 1834. Scarcely had the news of Kelly's death at
Rome reached MacHale when his mentor Dr Waldron died unexpectedly on
20 May 1834. As his coadjutor MacHale succeeded him. Shortly after his
funeral MacHale attended a meeting at Tuam to select and propose a new
archbishop. After much discussion the priests of the diocese selected two
major candidates from north-Mayo parishes, MacHale from Ballina, and, his
contemporary at Maynooth, Bernard Burke, dean of the archdiocese of Tuam
and parish priest of Westport. The third candidate was the eighty-five year old
Archdeacon Nolan, vicar-capitular and parish priest of Balla.[15] Burke got one
vote more than MacHale,[16] but MacHale was the choice of the bishops of
Tuam province, for the prestigious post as one of the four archbishops in
Ireland. MacHale triumphantly left his native diocese for his consecration as
archbishop of Tuam on 8 August 1834.

The archdiocese of Tuam extended over nearly 1,400,000 acres divided
into seven deaneries with fifty-one parishes. The deaneries of Ballinrobe,
Castlebar, Clifden, Claremorris, Dunmore, Tuam and Westport extended along
the west coast of Ireland from Achill island, in County Mayo, to Inisheer island
in Galway Bay and inland to Mount Bellew. MacHale faced a daunting task of
establishing a vibrant Roman Catholic organisation within his archdiocese.
Under Archbishop Kelly the diocese had established good central administration
but enormous diocesan development was essential. Dean Burke wrote that
MacHale continued his predecessor's church embellishment programme.

I don't know a thatched chapel in the County Mayo but one, which is
very large, and always kept in good repair. Some of the country chapels
are not ceiled, because they are boarded; Generally speaking there are
silver chalices in all the chapels in this diocese. Plated being changed,
but silver ones are being purchased every day. Archbishop examined
vestments, and all unbecoming vestments, cloths etc burnt.[17]

A church building, and refurbishment programme was well advanced but the
provision of schools needed urgent attention.

Archbishop Oliver Kelly favoured the national education system, even
though the people in the archdiocese of Tuam were predominantly Roman
Catholic.[18] MacHale watched its evolution and knew all the fears and hopes
entertained for it. He felt that the system was fraught with danger to the youth
of Ireland and he distrusted any system of a mixed-religion education. He
wanted denominational education funded by a state grant to each of the
Catholic bishops.[19] Other bishops, while having some misgivings about the
system, decided that their interests were being met by the inclusion of
Archbishop Daniel Murray of Dublin on the body of commissioners. Bishop
Doyle of Kildare and Leighlin wrote to his priests:

> Should bad men succeed the present commissioners, and attempt to
> corrupt the education of youth, we are not dumb dogs who know not
> how to bark; we can guard our flocks, and do so easily by the simple
> process of excluding the commissioners and their books and agents
> from our schools. We might by doing so forfeit the aid which they
> would, if the supposition were realised, be entitled to withhold, but in
> withholding it, they would be answerable to Parliament, to which we
> would also, have access.[20]

The Protestant bishops did not accept the commissioners' stance on religion.
In November 1836, Archbishop Trench, in a letter to Archdeacon Verschoyle,
vicar-general of Killala wrote, rather cryptically:

> for the present I would feel it prudent to take no step, in the hope that
> the primate may take a course in which all the clergy of Ireland shall
> unite, to give expression to the confirmation by experience of that
> unhallowed system of education, to which, in its infancy, they gave their
> unqualified dissent.[21]

From such enigmatic comments it is evident that he adopted a cautious attitude
towards the newly launched system of national education. The commissioners
of national education in Ireland aimed to be absolutely impartial in the matter
of religion, yet in pursuing that, they succeeded in alienating the bishops of

the very people whom they wished to educate. Many changes were made to the system over the next half a century before the churches, even grudgingly, totally accepted it. The national school system was a marvellous opportunity to make a concerted attack on illiteracy The Board of Education would 'establish and maintain a model school in Dublin and train teachers, some of whom may be already teaching, for country schools'.[22] The commissioners saw the well-trained schoolmaster

> whose conduct and influence must be highly beneficial in promoting morality, harmony and good order, in the country parts of Ireland; living in friendly habit with the people, not greatly elevated above them, but so provided for as to be able to maintain a respectable station; trained to good habits; identified in interest with the state, and therefore anxious to promote a spirit of obedience to lawful authority, we are confident that they would prove a body of the utmost value and importance in promoting civilisation and peace.[23]

Eight million persons lived in Ireland, with about 1,140,000 (or about a seventh of the whole) between the ages of seven and thirteen years. The government was satisfied that, at least, one half of that number would require the aid of national schools with an optimum size of 100 pupils per school. That meant that 5,000 national schools would serve the whole country. They envisaged a time span of nine years to achieve their target.[24] If we apply the same criteria for the provision of schools to the archdiocese, with its population of 370,000, then 260 schools would be needed. The enrolment figures show that a large part of the school-age population was outside the education system. In Clifden deanery only 12 per cent of the relative age cohort were enrolled. However, the impoverished population of parts of the archdiocese lived in remote areas, so to fully educate the people up to 300 schools were required.

Table 1. State of education, archdiocese of Tuam, 1834

DEANERY	% of school-age population enrolled as scholars
Ballinrobe	48
Castlebar	62
Claremorris	70
Clifden	12
Dunmore	66
Tuam	43
Westport	60

Source: *First report of the commissioners on public instruction 1835*, pp 46d–79d, HC 1835 [45], xxxiii, 806–839.

The United Kingdom government, in inaugurating the national education system, did not take cognisance of the fact that there were massive disparities of income within Ireland. It was inevitable that the more well-endowed landed families, many of whom were of a different religious persuasion to their tenants, would be required to subsidise the less well-off families. Yet, many of the heavily indebted landlords were not in financial control of their estates. For the system of national schools to succeed, the goodwill of the local clergy, landlords and people was essential. MacHale noted that the government's initial projection was 5,000 national schools, over a nine-year period. That amount would launch an effective attack on illiteracy. The actual provision of schools in Table 2 illustrates that the target figures were almost entirely abandoned.

Table 2. National Schools, Ireland, 1833–41

Year	Schools in operation	Pupils on roll '000	Total government grant £'000
1833	800	107	25
1834	1,000	140	20
1835	1,100	145	35
1836	1,180	153	50
1837	1,300	167	50
1838	1,385	170	50
1839	1,580	193	50
1840	1,980	232	57
1841	2,340	282	55

Source: Compiled from first to ninth reports, CNEI 1834–42.

Even if sufficient funds for education were available the home conditions of the scholars were heart-rendingly primitive. The clergy and landlords recognised that people were in dire need of relief from lives of unremitting toil and misery. The main task in life was to provide food and shelter for their families. One of their foremost problems was how to cope with the ever-increasing supply of labour, which, by the 1830s, greatly exceeded demand. The advent of the industrial age had catastrophic effects on the west of Ireland cottage industries of spinning and weaving home-produced wool and linen. The recurring partial crop failures ensured that the poor constantly hovered between subsistence and starvation. 'The rent' was the shield against eviction for both the landlord and tenant. Some times labour was exacted in lieu of rent. We get a picture of life in the archdiocese from the 1835 parliamentary inquiry into the state of the poor. A typical report on Glenamaddy, County Galway paints a very bleak picture of people living in intense poverty and deprivation:

The population is wholly agricultural and very numerous; their clothing tolerable; food very bad, and deficient in quantity, in bad seasons; bedding in general very bad; furniture, little or none; ventilation extremely bad.[25]

The landholders held the land with a sense of deference to the resident or non-resident landlord, or to his agent, since they were not leaseholders but tenants-at-will. Despite the absence of leases, the landlord was, in most cases, content to receive the rent with the minimum of contact with the tenants. The agents were paid a collection commission so, in their own interests, they maximised their incomes. In his evidence before the Devon Commission, at Castlebar on 31 July 1844, commissioner for oaths James Conry stated:

> Land was let for up to double its poor law valuation by auction, because the poor have no earthly means of turning their labour to any account, except by procuring land, and in consequence there is competition for every little patch of land that is to be let; generally speaking the land is let at a great deal more than its value.[26]

95 per cent of County Mayo farms were less than 15 acres[27] so the acquisition of even a garden-patch was imperative for survival.

Landlord and tenant relations were one of mutual dependency. The people were usually at the mercy of the landlord as James Tuke, an astute Quaker who was sent to Connacht to report on the famine, saw on his visit to the O'Donnel estate, in Burrishoole barony in north Mayo. He saw a thousand persons, mainly women, harvesting crops at 4d. per day for women and 8d. per day for men. O'Donnel had 2,500 acres of flax for which he paid the tenant £5–£7 per acre. In the open market the price prevailing was £15–£20 an acre. The breakdown of the costs of producing that flax:

Rent of one acre	£1. 10s.–£1. 15s.
Seed for one acre	£1. 5s.
2 diggings	£1. 8s.
+ county cess, taxes, manure.[28]	

There was little profit when sold to the landlord yet this might be attributed to his own personal indebtedness. Some of the estate owners were highly indebted on account of crop failures, marriage settlements and the penal laws, which came to an end a lifetime earlier. Lord John Russell, wrote:

> One of the greatest evils of Ireland is the nominal possession of estates by persons who have no means of improving them or doing them justice; they would be able, by selling a part, to make the rest more valuable.[29]

While O'Donnel is to be commended in giving work to so many people yet the people needed cash to augment the national schools grants applied for by their parish priest, James Hughes of Burrishoole, for sites donated by O'Donnel.

The dependency of people on their landlords was such that they eulogised them on occasion, such as the visit in September 1836 of Charles Henry, Viscount Dillon, who resided in Oxford England, to his County Mayo estate where he owned a vast portion of the diocese.[30] His agent, an Englishman, Strickland, treated the tenants in a humane and dignified manner. The *Mayo Telegraph* tells how thousands of his tenants awaited Dillon's arrival with bonfires blazing as he made his procession into Ballaghderreen town for a formal dinner. In reply to a toast in his honour, he said 'it will be my greatest happiness to cultivate relations of mutual regard between my tenants, my neighbours and myself.'[31] Viscount Dillon was one of the landlords who sought to advance the education of his tenantry much to the chagrin of Dr MacHale. He was a first cousin of Dominic Browne of Castlemagarrett – Lord Oranmore and Browne – with whom, as we shall see later, MacHale was a trustee of national schools in 1838.

Practical problems faced parents and scholars. It was difficult to be responsive in school when one shared a one-roomed mud cabin often with three generations of people who all ate, slept and lived together.

> It was not unusual for the rain to drip through the thatched roof so that one half of its small open space is continually in sop. There was one apartment in which the whole family of grown up young men and women eat and sleep. The members of the household commonly rest upon straw or heather, laid on the floor, covered by a blanket, if it be in possession, and wearing apparel of several sleepers. The pig – the never absent guest – a cow if there be one – and occasionally a few fowl occupy the same chamber at night.[32]

That house was typical of the majority of houses in the Tuam archdiocese. The lowest class (class 4), described above, decreased by up to 85 per cent between 1841 and 1851. With the massive annihilation of the poor, and middle-class emigration, the overall number of houses (excluding Aran) decreased by between one-fifth and two-fifths. People could see that a way out of their plight was through education but getting an education meant an unaccustomed reliance on cash. Local fund-raising was essential as aid from the government was limited to two-thirds of the estimated costs of enclosing the site and building and furnishing the school. Each step that the applicant took: the provision of a site, the trusteeship of the completed schoolhouse, the employment of a teacher, all had to be approved by the commissioners. Each applicant had to satisfy the board that the schoolhouse would be kept in repair. Further ongoing provision had to be made towards a permanent salary, to augment the allowance towards salary made by the government. The commissioners aimed to give pupils the fundamentals of literacy. They stated – 'we consider that the schools under us should tend as far as practicable to bring forward an intelligent class of farm-labourers and servants.'[33] To make the schools more economically relevant they attached farms to some schools and, in 1838, introduced agriculture to the curriculum. Sewing, knitting and embroidery for girls and agriculture or other industrial instruction for boys could be taught. The board had complete control over the content of the curriculum. It published its own school books, thus giving uniformity of instruction, then issued free stock to each school every four years, with the remainder available at a little over half cost price. They were designed as five consecutive books of lessons designed to equip the pupil with basic knowledge on geography, grammar, morals, scripture and environment – as well as reading skills. In a school application for Kilmaine in 1834 the parish priest, James Browne, wrote:

> The books issued by the Board, such as came under my observation, are well adapted to promote the benevolent object of the national system by giving the poor a moral and well regulated plan of education.[34]

The Roman Catholic diocese of Tuam was 84 per cent of the size of the Protestant diocese of Tuam because the Protestant diocese was coextensive with the Roman Catholic dioceses of both Tuam and Galway. Tuam was the cathedral city for both denominations. Power Le Poer Trench (1770–1839) was the last Protestant archbishop of Tuam. A son of the first Earl Clancarty, he was a member of a very wealthy and influential east Galway family. On his mother's side Trench was a nephew of Luke Gardiner, Lord Mountjoy, who was a major land developer in the north-east sectors of Dublin city. His brothers and sisters married into some of the richest and most influential of the County Galway gentry – the Dillons of Clonbrock, Elwoods of Ashford Castle.[35] His brother-in-law William Gregory was Under Secretary at Dublin Castle.

MacHale and Trench felt that the teaching of religion was being compromised but decided to wait and see how the system would work out in practice. People flocked to where free schooling was available, even if it was not by Roman Catholics, but by scripture readers sent from England:

> Schools have been found to be the most effective mode of gaining admittance to the people; and the rapid success which has marked the work may be traced, in a great degree, to the application of this means.[36]

In the years 1821–41, despite its remoteness, both the population and the number of houses of that most western barony of Ballynahinch, increased by a massive 82 per cent. The state of Clifden deanery with 45,000 persons, many of them eking out an existence in extreme poverty, is particularly worth noting. The population was overwhelmingly Roman Catholic, with 2 per cent members of the established church, and less than 1 per cent of other Christian denominations. There was one place of worship for every 170 non-Catholics as against one place of worship for every 3,492 Catholics.[37] Three clergymen ministered to 590 Protestants whereas there was only one priest for every 3,000 Catholics in the deanery.[38] This dearth of priests was a very important factor in the growth of proselytism as it led to the acceptance by educationally deprived Catholics of education in non-Catholic schools. Trench, a humane pastor, was passionately interested in the conversion of the Roman Catholics through Bible study. Irish was still the vernacular of more than half the people, so in order to achieve his aim of making the Bible more readily available he was involved in translating it to Irish.[39] He decided to counter the national schools system by forming with his clergy, in 1832, the Tuam Diocesan Education Society. His own clergymen were appointed as inspectors to oversee the work of his schools. They had a proselytising role since they were required to preach the word of God, in the Irish language, to the mainly Roman Catholic adults of the area. In 1834, their schools were at Achill, Ardagh, Ardygommon, Ayle, Ballinlough, Ballinonagh, Belcarra, Breaffy, Burrishoole, Carrahowly, Cloondehamper, Tuam, Clifden, Crossboyne, Kilmaine, Lessavally, Nappagh, Slingen, Tully and Westport, that is mostly in the western part of the diocese. Trench, the last Protestant Archbishop of Tuam, died in 1839.

Relations between the Protestant and Roman Catholic clergy of Tuam diocese were usually amicable. MacHale plainly held no personal animosity against individual Protestants but was implacably opposed to what he perceived as proselytism. As we noted earlier he was a regular visitor to the duke of Leinster and a friend of the gentry of Connacht of both denominations. In fact he welcomed them to his cathedral. In an account of the Corpus Christi procession in Tuam in 1847, attended by MacHale and some of his suffragan bishops, by the nobility and gentry, 'several highly respectable Protestants were accommodated with seats in the sacred edifice and along the line the procession was to move'.[40] Some years later in 1851, people in Tuam were incensed by allegations made about local religious animosity. A public meeting was told that ' . . . Archbishop Trench thatched the houses of the poor and ministered to their wants, irrespective of religion'.[41]

Trench was succeeded, in 1839, by Thomas Plunket, the eldest son of William, Baron Plunket, Chancellor of Ireland 1830–41. Thomas, married in 1819, Louisa Foster of County Louth, whose kinsman Vere Foster was, in 1868, to play a major role in the formation of the Irish National Teachers' Organisation. In 1839, Thomas Plunket became bishop of the newly united diocese of Tuam, Killala and Achonry. In the same year the Diocesan Education Societies of the Established Church united to form the Church Education Society. Its aim was to provide and maintain schools for Protestants outside the national education system. Plunket could afford to remain aloof from the national schools' system as he had the resources of the gentry and the well-to-do families of his own and his predecessor's persuasion to rely upon in the formation of schools, which were open to children of all faiths. In the highly charged atmosphere they made inroads into illiteracy. By 1849 the society had about a quarter of the number of pupils of the national school system on its rolls and of these one-third were Roman Catholic.[42] One of the most persistent proselytisers was Alexander Dallas, an English clergyman who founded the Irish Church Mission with the avowed purpose of weaning Roman Catholics to Protestantism by providing them with schools. He initially zoned in on the Atlantic sea-board part of the archdiocese where he used 'maps from the 1841 census to show where ignorance was greatest ; there were two churches and four incumbents in sixty miles'.[43]

The Protestant leaders availed of the wealth of their congregations while MacHale had to rely on the voluntary services of the religious orders. The Franciscan Brothers were an obvious choice since their headquarters at Mountbellew was already within MacHale's jurisdiction. In 1835 MacHale requested the Brothers to begin a monastery and school, in one of the wildest and most uncultivated parts of Ireland at Roundstone in Connemara.[44] The school was grant-aided at £60 by the board, but in order to preserve the purely Roman Catholic ethos of the school, the salary of John O'Flaherty was £6 a year from the parish priest and about £8 a year from the pupils with no contribution from the board.[45] MacHale obviously hoped that that was to be the forerunner for the funding arrangements of several such schools. The commissioners welcomed applications from combined Catholic and non-Catholic applicants, both clerical and lay. The composition of groups who applied, illustrates the circumstances of the local landlords, and the interaction between the clergy of both denominations within individual parishes.

Each application tells its own story. The provision of a local subscription towards the national schools posed many problems. Some parishes, while appreciating education, were paralysed by lack of family income from agriculture, trade or fishing. The parish priest of Kilgeever (Louisburg), James Dwyer, said that the local fishery had failed and fishermens' families were living in total poverty. The seas were teeming with fish, but the fishermen had a hazardous existence for the want of safe harbours.[46] One of his parish schools was held in a threshing barn at Kill and he requested furniture as the children sat on stones by the wall in his school at Fallduff.[47] Another north Mayo priest, Peter Ward parish priest of the 120 square mile parish of Aughagower, ministered to 8,000 impoverished parishioners. The commissioners looked favorably on his plea as he was granted, in 1832, salary and money towards desks for the buildings he was already using at Aughagower, Cushinkeel, Triangle and Lanmore.[48] Other parishes with early associations with the board were Moyrus parish, on the southern shore of Connemara, with schools at Ballinafad, Roundstone and Moyrus. James Hughes parish priest at Burrishoole, a tenant of O'Donnel in west Mayo, got simple school houses (30 feet by 20 feet) to replace small 12 feet by 14 feet schools with stone seats, conducted under hedge school conditions, at Newport, Carrickahawla, Derryloughan, Doontrusk, Letterlough, Mulranny, Newfield, Rossturk and Trienbeg. Each was grant aided at £71. 19s. 10d.[49] It was indeed a massive undertaking in such a wild area of County Mayo beneath Nephin mountains. Island people appreciated the benefits that would flow from schools so early applications came from the parish priests of Inishturk, Clare island and Inniskea.[50] From windswept, treeless Inisboffin, six miles off Cleggan, John Griffin parish priest wanted 2.5 tons of timber to be shipped, with carriage paid from Westport, for a new school.[51] The number of pupils on roll in national schools within the archdiocese grew steadily so that by 1834 County Galway had 1,300 males and 800 females, and County Mayo had 3,300 males and 1,780 females on roll.[52] Thirty years later, Henry M'Manus, a Presbyterian minister in Connemara, commented:

> The present improved system of education has imparted to the peasantry an increased desire for it. We say, an increased for it, for they have always appreciated it. The most ignorant of them have always respected learning in others, and earnestly coveted it for their children.[53]

In keeping with their non-denominational culture the commissioners did not wish to have a national school in a place used for religious worship. In many parishes the chapel, as the only fairly substantial building in the locality, was used as a schoolhouse during the week. Within the first year of the new system an application was lodged by the enthusiastic, energetic Richard Gibbons parish priest Castlebar, (former professor of humanities at Maynooth College), for a new school in Breaffy parish to replace the school held in the parish chapel. It was estimated to cost £80. 3s. 4d. The commissioners granted £50 on condition that a schoolhouse would not be built within the confines of the church land. The builder Thomas Comber built a substantial house 48 feet long by 18 feet wide by 9 feet high with two feet thick rubble masonry walls roofed with Bangor slates.[54] It must have caused much comment in that rural part of County Mayo where the population lived mainly in small cabins. Thirty miles away, at Cong, the school was removed from the chapel to two small rooms in the local pub where:

> whiskey is sold and having a signboard to that effect outside it. The rooms, tables and forms are used for whiskey shop on fair and leisure days. The only alternative place was to hold school in the chapel as the parish priest wished but they were afraid that it wouldn't be funded.[55]

In 1834, about 40 per cent of chapels in the archdiocese of Tuam were used as schoolrooms during the week. The basic curriculum was reading, writing and arithmetic. Bookkeeping was popular too (table 3).

Table 3. Schools held in chapels in archdiocese of Tuam, 1834

Deanery	Parish	Chapel	Teacher	Average daily attendance	Extra subjects
Ballinrobe	Cong	Cong	Richard Corbett	70	Bookkeeping
Ballinrobe	Kilmolara	Kilmolara	Pat Hessian	50	Bookkeeping
Ballinrobe	Partree	Ballybannon	David Deane	30	
Ballinrobe	do	Partree	J&R Walsh	70	
Ballinrobe	Ross	Fairhill	Patrick Fallon	50	
Castlebar	Ballintubber Abbey		Patrick Hindley	40	Bookkeeping Surveying
Castlebar	do		Austin Ryder	40	
Castlebar	do	Killevalla	Thomas M'Gough	60	
Castlebar	Ballyhane	Ballyhane	John Kelly	40	
Castlebar	Burriscarra	Burriscarra	Michael McDonald	60	Bookkeeping
Claremorris	Annagh	Tulrahan	Peter Burke	60	Bookkeeping
Claremorris	Bekan	Bekan	James Doyle	30	
Claremorris	Claremorris	Barnacarroll	Timothy Boyle	90	Geography
Dunmore	Kilkerrin	Kilkerrin	John Creig	70	
Dunmore	Killtullagh	Granlahan	John Geoghegan	70	
Tuam	Annaghdown	Annaghdown	Malachi Hardagan	90	
Tuam	Corrofin	Corrofin	Pat Molloy	18	
Tuam	Donoghpatrick		Michael Walsh	70	Bookkeeping
Tuam	Headford	Headford	Thomas Connolly	50	
Tuam	Headford	Kilkilvery	Wm. Shaughnessy	80	
Tuam	Kilbannon	Kilbannon	Daniel O'Beirne	60	
Tuam	Kilconla	Kilconla	Wm. Connolly	60	
Tuam	Killeany	Cloughanower	Ml. Joyce	60	
Tuam	Killererin	Killererin	Patrick Horan	60	
Tuam	Liskeevy	Ballyglass	Patrick Maxwell	40	
Tuam	Moore	Cloonfad	Thomas Kenney	60	
Tuam	Moore	Moore	James Gavin	40	
Westport	Kilmeen	Kilmeen	John Kenny	80	Bookkeeping

Source: *First report of the commissioners on public instruction*, p. 45d–73d HC 1835 (45), xxxiii, 606–633

Schools varied in their fitness to house pupils. In a survey more than twenty years later, in 1858, Patrick Joseph Keenan, a local schools inspector, wrote:

> As regards the character and condition of the buildings, it may be seen that nearly half the schools are classed as good, and a little more than a fourth as fair; and considering the circumstances of the country at the time when most of these buildings were erected, their condition may be looked upon as satisfactory. Two per cent of the schools are still,

2. Cabin used for school at Glan, *c.*1850

however, wretched hovels – structures under the roof of which it is lamentable to have to gather together as many children as constitute a school; the means of ventilation are so bad, the lighting so imperfect, and the earthen floors damp and unhealthy.[56]

The inability of people to pay their share meant that the amount of the budget spent on actual schools in Connacht was about half what could reasonably have been anticipated – in fact the government stood convicted, according to MacHale, of not having allocated to Connacht its share of available funds.[57] The national school patrons of Connacht had contributed £2,296 as their one-third of the cost of school buildings. This was decried as being roughly equal to the £2,490 expended on the model school in Dublin.[58] In his hard hitting, thorough elucidation MacHale suggested to Lord John Russell that

> adopting the principle of a just economy in conducting the National Education system your Lordship will get rid at once of the useless humbug of a metropolitan model school and the long suite of clerks and inspectors. While all this annual expenditure is going on let not the people of the provinces be derided as heretofore with the answer – there are no funds.

He hoped that no Chancellor who grants funds will call it a grant for the education of the poor in Ireland.[59] Further letters in the public press continued. In May 1838 Russell advocated a grant towards denominational education maintaining for Protestants a right to be educated in their own principles, yet he was ready to devote any particular sum to Roman Catholics in any general instruction.[60] Thirty-five years later denominational grants were conceded. Schools which were so substandard in the 1858 report were probably schools which were in use long before the government grants became available, and which were only fitted out at government expense. MacHale carefully studied each annual report of the commissioners of national education in Ireland. He noted that the government's initial projection was 5,000 national schools, over a nine-year period. That amount would launch an effective attack on illiteracy. The actual provision of schools in Table 2 illustrates that the target figures were almost entirely abandoned.[61]

MacHale was aware that government funds were diverted to core projects, so, even where people were able to pay their share the grant was not available. The main project was the acquisition of a suitably prestigious headquarters, in central Dublin, for the commissioners of national education in Ireland. They decided on Tyrone House, formerly the town house of the marquess of Waterford. When he decided to sell his exquisite town house, designed a century earlier by the noted architect of Carton House and Leinster House, Richard Castle,[62] the British Government bought it for £6,750 in 1834.[63] It is still used as the Department of Education. Staff were recruited at salaries in keeping with the opulence of their surroundings.[64] Each board meeting decided on remuneration for even the most modest posts, at rates that were very much out of line with the annual salary of £8 they initially allowed the teachers.

Salary scales, introduced in 1839, were to be regarded as gratuities in support of payments from parents and from parish funds. As we saw earlier there were great disparities between the amounts rendered from other sources. The popularity, and possibly the effectiveness, of a teacher may be gauged from the local school fees advanced in Burrishoole parish. The only female teacher in the parish, Mrs Ferris in Newport female school, had an annual salary of £8 from the board and £14. 10s. in local subscriptions from a population of over 1,200 persons in the well-known grain exporting port. Newport parents, with a well-developed linen manufacturing and trading industry, were dilatory in supplementing the £8 paid to the local teachers by the government with £3 school-fees to Thomas Ryder and £1. 15s. to Edward Wallace of Trienbeg. This was supplemented by £1 per annum from the marquis of Sligo.[65]

MacHale allowed the clergy to accept government money under the commissioners of national education in Ireland regulations, from the system's beginning until 1838, without any audible protest. Several parishes which had compliant gentry had pupils housed and taught in adequate surroundings. In late 1837 MacHale changed his public attitude to outright condemnation of the National Schools. The change of tactic was thoroughly discussed by the bishops of Ireland assembled in Dublin for their annual general meeting on 23 January 1839. Following a full and frank discussion on the national education system they found no inconsistency with articles of faith or morals. They would continue to monitor the system and, if adequate means were placed at it's disposal, the commissioners of national education in Ireland would confer substantial benefits on this country.[66] MacHale and his suffragan bishops did not agree with the majority of their fellow bishops. They continued to argue that a denominational system was the only way forward, so MacHale implemented his personal convictions and one by one his schools were closed, teachers were unemployed or reverted to hedge school conditions and parents were perplexed. The commissioners wished schools to remain in conjunction with the board so communications continued with individual school managers in the archdiocese. The commissioners adopted a hard line and clerical managers were dismissed but lay managers could be appointed.

MacHale's early years in Tuam archdiocese 1834–9 coincided with the first decade of Catholic Emancipation. He devoted his energies and finances towards showing the people that the Catholic church could regain pre-eminence in Irish affairs. His splendid cathedral, at Tuam, was a harbinger of greater times in the future, and slated churches graced every parish in the diocese. MacHale and Trench were optimistic that their tenacity and stubbornness would achieve schools according to their wishes. Trench, an elderly man in declining health, saw his Tuam Diocesan Education Society's schools flourish. There are many suppositions as to what might have happened if, within a decade, the great Famine had not occurred. The great Famine wrought incalculable damage to the infrastructure of the diocese. MacHale challenged the government on other issues such as the bequests bills and the universities. More importantly the diocese suffered through the deaths of some very able priests, politicians and other leaders of society. The British government would, sooner rather than later, have to listen to MacHale, but with the demise of some of his trusted friends such as his former Maynooth colleague, Martin Loftus, he lost the fellowship, rapport and wise counsel of his confidants.

The strangers came to teach them their ways

Religion for all denominations was of paramount importance in the lives of the people in the archdiocese of Tuam. John MacHale and Thomas Plunket, speaking in the name of religion, could exercise tremendous control because they spoke to the hearts and minds of people. In January 1839 MacHale departed from the bishops' consensus of opinion and voiced his outright opposition to the national schools. Kitson Clark, writing on the religious scene in Ireland and England claimed that:

> It might not be too extravagant a claim to say of the nineteenth century that probably in no other century, except the seventeenth and perhaps the twelfth, did the claims of religion occupy so large a part in the nation's life or did men speaking in the name of religion contrive to exercise so much power.[1]

The Famine of the 1840s and the void created by the closure of the national schools in the archdiocese gave an opening to Protestant evangelists to make headway with Protestant mission schools. In Achill, in 1835, Rev. Edward Nangle set up an independent Protestant settlement at Dugort. He solicited funds for schools while MacHale appealed for support for church building, still hopeful that government grants for purely Catholic national schools would be proffered.

> We beg to call a special notice to the island of Achill in which the Rev. Mr. Dwyer is making every exertion, aided by the zealous and benevolent to build two chapels. When it is known that the anti-Catholic bigoted set of fanatics, are trying every means to seduce the poor and ignorant in this place, it is confidently hoped that they will liberally subscribe to the genuine work of charity and religion.[2]

The Irish Church Missions gained a foothold in Achill and became an important part of the missionary work of the Protestant diocese of Tuam. In Achill schools were founded at Cashel, Dugort, Rockfield, Shraheen and at Meelan training school where astronomy, geography, logic, science, scripture history and doctrine were on the curriculum. In the meantime, MacHale expended the limited means at his disposal in countering the advances in education generated by the evangelists. Castlebar chapel, the parish of the zealous Richard Gibbons parish priest, was his chosen venue, in March 1840, to announce that he had cut off all connection between the national schools in Tuam archdiocese and the board of education. He called on the people of Castlebar to 'subscribe liberally towards the support of schools where Roman Catholics would be morally and intellectually educated under the immediate superintendence of the Catholic bishops and clergy'.[3]

MacHale possibly saw Tuam town as a model for what was attainable, in the absence of government aid, throughout his diocese. It had a well-established education system. The Franciscan Brothers had an excellent school for boys,[4] which was a model school for the Galway portion of the diocese.[5] By 1843 it had expanded to 400 pupils:

> who without any check from any anti-Catholic quarter on their cherished practices of devotion, are trained, by able masters, in reading, writing, bookkeeping, and many of them in the higher branches of mathematics.[6]

In 1835 the Presentation Sisters opened a free school where they taught literary, industrial, and religious subjects to 200–300 girls.[7] Architect Henry Hart was commissioned to design a large convent, which was built immediately after the Famine.[8] In 1846 a convent of Mercy augmented that group of buildings.

> The convent, the cathedral, St Jarlath's college, and the archbishop's residence are all contiguous to each other and convey to the mind an image of those times, though not an adequate one, when the Catholic church with its subsidiary advantages blessed our once happy country.[9]

The Roman Catholic people of Tuam archdiocese suffered many setbacks as they tried to emerge from dire poverty. Most of these, such as the 1839 famine, were outside their control. At this time, the emerging Young Ireland movement advocated that Irishmen, irrespective of religion, should join together to seek control of their own destiny by seeking independence from England. They welcomed, with reservations, the national schools:

> The national schools are a vast improvement on anything hitherto in this country, but still have great many faults. From the miserably small grant, the teachers are badly paid, and therefore hastily and meagerly educated. We have spoken to pupils and masters who know nothing of Ireland beyond home. Until the national schools fall under national control the people must take diligent care to procure books on the history, men, language, music and manners of Ireland for their children[10]

When MacHale ordered the closure of the national schools in his diocese the controversial situation was immediately placed before Pope Gregory XVI.

Archbishop Daniel Murray of Dublin[11] and MacHale were invited to put their respective cases before Propaganda Fide. In spring 1840, MacHale sent his former Maynooth colleague, Martin Loftus, who was then parish priest, and manager of Dunmore national school, County Galway, to represent him at Rome.[12] Monsignor Paul Cullen, rector of the Irish College in Rome, on holidays in his native County Kildare in September 1840, wrote to Propaganda and suggested that the schools continue while safeguards could be built into the system in the future for the protection of religion in schools.[13] Cullen's assessment was noted and on 16 January 1841 Propaganda anticipated that its decision to let each bishop adjudge the national schools issue for his own diocese, would not fully please either side, so it asked the bishops to refrain from public controversy on the matter. The schools were accepted in Armagh, Cashel and Dublin ecclesiastical provinces. Paul Cullen was very well aware of his friend MacHale's misgivings towards the ethos of the national schools system, and how personally disappointing to him was the conclusion reached by Propaganda. A month later he wrote to MacHale and suggested that:

> By abstaining from discussing [in his Lenten pastoral] that question, everybody will admire your forbearance and you will have the evident merit of having attended literally to the instructions from Rome.[14]

MacHale conscientiously objected to the non-denominational grants and decided to be independent of government funding for education. His flock was most obviously desperately poor. Of course he did not know what would happen as the next decade unfolded, but, in hindsight, this would prove to be the worst possible time to reject government grants as the catastrophic Famine severely damaged the social structure. The numbers of Catholic people of substance diminished through death, emigration or bankruptcy. MacHale pondered his dilemma, and in 1842 thundered in his Lenten pastoral:

> We have heard with much pain that a few Protestant proprietors, some of them glorying in the very equivocal title of Liberals, have erected some houses, intended for schools, covering their bigotry under a show of regard for the education of people they have refused to grant leases of the smallest spots of land to the Catholic clergymen, either for schools or for chapels.[15]

The allegation that Protestant proprietors have refused to grant leases was certainly not wholly true. After 1839, their contributions to education were, as we shall see later, though repudiated by MacHale were generally approved of by his clergy. Times had certainly changed in the few years since MacHale had acted as trustee for Lord Oranmore and Browne's schools. MacHale was immensely confident that the Catholic gentry and merchants of Connacht would finance a scheme for education of the poor:

> Catholic schools are the only schools that are sanctioned by the archbishop within the archdiocese. Pious gentry are assisting him and the clergy with ample endowments. Some of the most opulent and respectable families in the diocese have pledged themselves to still further donations in land, in order to place for ever the authority of the bishop, in preserving for ever the faith of the young portion of his flock, beyond the reach of annoyance[16]

He resolutely tried to provide schools for his people, and he expected that such measures would probably be for a short period because, sooner rather than later, the government would see the wisdom of, and accede to, his demands. In an effort to inspire his supporters and promulgate the effects of their generosity the assertion continued:

> In the last account of the state of religious education in the archdiocese, authenticated by the signatures of their respective parish priests, more than 13,000 children were receiving the benefits of a purely Catholic education. Since then, from the zeal of the clergy, and the eagerness with which the young pant for an education imbued with the spirit of freedom – as regard the exercises of prayers at the commencement and end of studies, and the use of enlightened books of catholic devotion at all times – the numbers have considerably increased.[17]

Church collections for the work of church building and furnishing continued. In a diocese with over 400,000 persons and a potential school population of 55,000 an immense number of people were being deprived of both secular and religious education. Church attendance lessened still further during the Famine. MacHale realised that though his people were denied secular instruction it was imperative that catechiesis should continue. Every Sunday, confraternities of the Christian Doctrine, in most parishes, instructed hundreds of children in the approved catechisms, and promoted the circulation and perusal of religious books[18] as they prepared the people for the Sacraments. MacHale compiled a catechism in English and, to make it more accessible to the immense number of Irish-speaking Catholics, Martin Loftus translated it into Irish.[19] Loftus's catechism was placed before the bishops' meeting in Dublin on 11 November 1842. He was requested to publish a cheap edition. Each bishop pledged to take copies, with MacHale (he ordered 100 copies) commenting that it was for the 'more extensive diffusion of the genuine scriptures in the Irish language with approved notes and comments.'[20] In the autumn of 1842 Louisa Moore of the Moore Catholic landed family at Ballyglass, County Mayo, with the approval of her friend MacHale, had compiled, published and promised to circulate, gratuitously, a thousand copies of her extracts from scripture.[21] MacHale was satisfied that

> Never shall we hand over to the enemies of our faith the selection of
> the masters or the books for the instruction of the rising generation;
> and were we to do so the youth of our diocese would be now under
> apostate teachers[22]

Huge numbers were confirmed when normal conditions were restored in the
years following the Famine. MacHale confirmed 1,000 at Cong in July 1854[23]
and 1,300 at Milltown, Ballindine and Aughagower the following September.[24]

The public and private murmuring of the gentry and clergy show the
angst caused by MacHale's interdict. Priests and people were dismayed when,
in 1839, MacHale instructed his clergy to spurn the national schools grants.
The gentry, too, were caught up in a web of intrigue in their efforts to
advance the education of their mainly Roman Catholic tenants. All worked
under the constraints imposed on them by the diocesan authorities. Many,
such as Richard Gibbons,[25] at Castlebar, quickly realised how valuable and
necessary the grants were to their hard pressed people. He had accepted one
of the first grants for school buildings at Breaffy in January 1833. Among the
schools opened by Gibbons were Driminacahill (Ballyhane) where Colonel
Edward Browne leased a site rent-free for 'as lasting as the purposes of
education'[26] and G.M. Sheridan leased a site at Derrylea.[27] His other schools
were at Snugboro, Breaffy, Aglish, Burrin, Cogula and Clonkeen.[28] Following
MacHale's sermon at Castlebar, Gibbons, a very concerned and educated pastor,
decided to camouflage his involvement by appointing lay school managers.
Catholic laymen Michael Clarke and Stephen Burke were his correspondents.
Hundreds of people had attended the schools over the previous decade.
Schools inspector McDonnell communicated with the parish priest and
several of the townspeople. He reported to the commissioners:

> The school is under a parochial committee chosen by Rev. Richard
> Gibbons PP. The Protestant clergyman opposes the system – the
> Roman Catholic clergyman approves of it. They are all anxious to have
> the school placed under the national board.[29]

The clergy were clearly divided. Some of the Roman Catholics, while out-
wardly concurring with MacHale, were reluctant to deprive their people of
an education. Gibbons had tried to find a method of continuing education
but MacHale, in his total opposition to the national schools, did not countenance any collusion, so he temporarily suspended him from his priestly duties.
Throughout the Tuam diocese priests on the one hand and the Protestant
ministers on the other were in a dilemma. Many of them probably found
great difficulty in conscientiously obeying their respective bishops. The
commissioners welcomed joint applications for schools but sometimes they
had to negotiate with one denomination.

The gentry, both Roman Catholic and Protestant, saw as businessmen the advantages to be gained for their tenantry in availing of government grants for education. They would hire Catholic teachers for children who were predominantly Catholics. They would adhere rigidly to the rules as entrusted to the commissioners for national education. Members of the Blake, Lynch, Moore and Browne families, Rev. Sir Francis Blosse Lynch of Castle Carra (a brother-in-law of Thomas Plunket Protestant bishop of Tuam, Killala and Achonry), the earl of Clanricard in County Galway and his County Mayo relations the marquess of Sligo, Lord Oranmore and Browne, and Lord Dillon set up national schools. Blosse Lynch crossed the religious divide when he gave a perpetual lease for a school site at Carnacon to John Kirby parish priest of Burriscarra.[30] A few years later, in the application for another Blosse Lynch school at Balla in 1845 schools' inspector J.J. O'Carroll reported 'the Roman Catholic clergyman does not wish to support the national school as his bishop is opposed to them'. The marquess of Sligo met the same rebuff when he leased a further site at Lehinch and contributed the full local contribution of one-third of the costs. Rev. T. Hardiman wrote to Giles Eyre, rector at Kilmeena, in 1844:

> The ordinary of this diocese having unequivocally avowed his disapprobation of the national system of education it is my duty to discountenance any attempt to introduce it into this parish. I could not and will not suffer any Catholic children to be educated by Mr Browne.[31]

At Carranamanister Ballyhaunis the Augustinian Friars gave a national school site rent-free. The rector refused to sign the application form on the instructions of Dr Plunket, stating that the national board had mutilated the Scriptures.[32]

Some parishes did not join the national school system until after MacHale's death in 1881. However, the story of schools in the parishes of Ballyhaunis, Bekan, Claremorris and Knock may be seen as a microcosm of the educational scene in many parishes throughout the Tuam diocese. The story begins in 1838, when the newly created Lord Oranmore and Browne leased sites for ninety nine years and donated the total local contributions of one-third of the building costs for schools at Ballindine, Lisduff (Scardane) and Ballaghfarna.[33] He appointed MacHale and Patrick Mullins, the local parish priest, as trustees for the schools at Ballindine and Claremorris parishes.[34] When MacHale issued his interdict in 1839 Claremorris parish had a predominantly Roman Catholic population with 8,822 Catholics and 181 Protestants. Despite his prohibition the schools persisted and were augmented by the largess of Oranmore and Browne's cousin Lord Dillon, who as we have already seen wished to cultivate relations of 'mutual regard between my tenants, my neighbours and myself'.[35] His agent, Strickland went ahead with schools for 1,500 pupils in the parishes of Ballyhaunis, Bekan, Claremorris and Knock. Strickland proactively consulted the local clergy and recorded the comments of priests and rectors. He had his lordship grant school leases at Larganboy, Polecapiel,[36] Crupard – 'the Roman Catholic clergyman, though he does not publicly interfere, would wish much national schools in this parish',[37] Carrowmore, Knock, Clonboy, Ballyhaunis, Bruff (Cloghooley), Knockatubber, Ballinastanford, Cahir and Churchfield.[38] Education documents note that, at Bekan – 'the Roman Catholic clergyman does not wish to take a prominent part in the establishment of national schools as it is in Tuam archdiocese'.[39] The words 'does not wish to take a prominent part' do not denote total disinterest or obstruction. The consequence of the implementation of that policy of 'mutual regard' meant that, fifty years later in 1891, Bekan parish recorded the highest level of literacy in the archdiocese at 81 per cent for boys and 76 per cent for girls.[40]

Were the priests divided amongst themselves, or did they seek to appease MacHale by their public pronouncements? It is difficult to divine if the parish priest and curate worked in harmony in relation to the Claremorris schools. Here again the education archival files and contemporary newspaper accounts differ. The commissioners' files state – 'the Protestant clergyman is opposed to it. The Roman Catholic approves of it but will not take any part in conducting the schools'.[41] Yet, the local paper recorded a most vicious verbal attack on Lord Dillon and his agent at Claremorris and Barnacarroll chapels. Did the parish priest who 'approves' of the schools, concur with the local curate Thomas Haddican when he denounced their national schools, and castigated their financial supporters as well as those sending their children to them? The people were determined that people power would prevail in bringing them out of ignorance, so they showed their disapproval of MacHale by walking out of the chapels as Haddican lambasted them.[42] People were perplexed. They turned to other community leaders when their priests spurned them. In the case of the ten year old school at Clonkeen, Castlebar, the local curate Patrick Hanly turned out the scholars and locked the doors. Shocked and frightened, the people went to the home of a local landlord, Dominic Browne, Greenhills, to state their case and to beg him to apply to the board for aid promising that all national school books, except Scripture extracts, would be used. The Scripture extracts were not compulsory so when books for 100 children were received, the school with teacher Andrew Collins reopened fifteen months later.[43]

Religious orders of men and women were establishing themselves as providers of a Catholic education in various parts of the country.[44] Now MacHale decided to solicit aid from the Roman Catholic gentry in inviting the religious women into his archdiocese. The Roman Catholic established national schools were closed, the Church Education Society was thriving and it was imperative to have many Catholic schools to provide a Catholic education. The Sisters of Mercy were to become of major importance in the diffusion of Catholic education in the diocese. Their foundress Catherine McAuley was present at the elevation of MacHale to the diocese of Killala in 1825. She was then, with some friends, helping less privileged members of society. Ten years later she formalised her community, and Pope Gregory XIV finally approved the order of the Sisters of Mercy just months before her death on 10 November 1841. The Sisters of Mercy in Carlow were invited by Dean Bernard Burke to start a girls' school at Westport. Burke was described as 'middle-aged, middle-sized figure, rustyish black coat, hessian boots, white stockings, good humoured, loud-speaking face, frequent Lundyfoot snuff'.[45] Would he as archbishop have led the diocese towards mass literacy? With his 'good humored, loud-speaking face' he was a man more in touch with his people than MacHale was, yet the bishops of the province of Tuam passed him over in favour of MacHale. As we shall see, ten years later he was still suffering much soul-searching in his obedience to MacHale. Meanwhile, the Roman Catholic gentry answered MacHale's call for assistance to enable his Franciscans to expand and educate the boys and young men. Martin Joseph Blake MP aided one of the first national schools in County Galway at Brierfield, and then set up the Franciscans at Brooklodge in Kilmoylan parish. Clifden and Roundstone monasteries were in the far west part of County Galway. A model school was needed for County Mayo so Mr Hardiman, historian of Galway and collector and publisher of *Ancient Irish minstrelry*, made a donation of ten acres of land in perpetuity at Errew, Ballyhean.[46] By 1842 the masonary work was complete, and fit to receive the roof, and the *Catholic Directory* recorded that 'with the assistance of God the two wings will be covered in before Christmas'.[47]

> Errew schools are now opened and the spaciousness of the school rooms, the loftiness of the walls, the correctness of the maps with which they are covered, and the acquirements of the masters who instruct the crowds of children who are flocking to this monastic association of piety and knowledge, not forgetting a splendid and well assorted library, would do credit to a country where the natural and holy alliance between religion and science has not, as in ours, been attempted to be divorced.[48]

Famine threw the school building programme into disarray. Destitution continued to be a recurring theme of countless official inquiries and visitors' reports. They portrayed the people of the mainly agricultural archdiocese living an abject poverty-stricken life. They could barely withstand one poor season but their main food source, the potato crop, failed annually from 1846 to 1848. Many of the wealthiest local landlords did not contribute to the relief funds. Some left their mansions in the care of agents and caretakers and left the country areas for their town houses or London quarters. Others claimed that they only considered their own tenants. MacHale was outraged by the amount of rent extracted from his starving people. While he may have rejected grants for education he was infuriated by the cessation of public works in Autumn 1846. MacHale to Lord John Russell, the prime minister:

You might as well issue an edict of general starvation as stop the supplies that the feeble creatures are striving to earn with the sweat of their brows. The pittance doled out this year for their relief would form but a small item in the millions abstracted without any return by absentees whom the Irish legislature would have kept at home to fulfil the duties as well as to enjoy the benefits of prosperity.[49]

In September 1846 the waxen faces of school children alarmed the teachers. Letters from the archdiocese inundated the government. People were appalled at the sight of another blighted potato crop. Joseph Kilgariff, the teacher at Balla, saw the fear and terror in the faces of parents all around him as 'meal of every description has risen within the last week . . . three prices for what provisions they are capable of purchasing'.[50] Eugene Coyne parish priest of Ballyhaunis witnessed the murmuring of these 'hungry, half naked persons, after having pawned their clothes to purchase a stone of meal and could not get it'.[51] MacHale appealed to his fellow bishops internationally to augment the diminishing resources of Tuam diocese, as he sought to mitigate and assuage the misery of the people. Inevitably, deaths from neglect began from the lack of food and heat. Within a few months, Dean Bernard Burke of Westport was devastated and depressed at the draconian methods used in rate collections:

From the manifest neglect of our devoted barony of Murrisk it would appear that our peaceful and enduring demeanor is to be rewarded by dragoons and infantry, powder ball and bayonets. Before another week the influence of the Catholic clergy is gone, hitherto so happily and effectually exercised. After next Sunday I fear hunger, starvation and death will prostrate all human influences, lay or clerical.[52]

Strickland, Lord Dillon's agent and manager of ten national schools, again rescued his tenants, by using his schools as food distribution centres, when he bought meal to distribute to parents and scholars.[53] The Franciscan Brothers accepted with gratitude aid offered by the British Association and the general Central Relief Committee, to give school children one substantial meal a day each during the worst of the Famine.[54] Almost all the people in the archdiocese received food rations at sometime during that period.

The diocese lost some of its best priests and Protestant clergy from fever and emigration to the colonies. Among the dead were MacHale's friend Martin Loftus of Dunmore; and Richard Gibbons of Castlebar, both very committed and able parish priests. Loftus was born in the same village, Lavallyroe Ballyhaunis, as the president (1845–9) of St Jarlath's College Tuam, Anthony O'Regan. O'Regan emigrated to St Louis, and within a few years was consecrated as third bishop of Chicago.[55] Loftus left an account of his people in May 1847:

How wretched are our prospects and some months before us and not a morsel of native food amongst us; almost all employment in Poor Works suspended; the streets filled with expectations of labour, and none to employ them; and yet the patience and forbearance under such privation. Such a people deserve better treatment.[56]

Three months later Loftus was dead. The Castlebar newspaper, the *Connaught Telegraph*, 20 May 1847, headline read 'Who shall go next?' It announced the deaths from fever of Patrick Pounder rector of Westport, Robert Potter Protestant clergyman, Louisburg, Dr Hamilton, Ballinrobe and Dr Jordan of Castlebar. Other contemporary newspapers detailed the deaths of local members of parliament Sir John Burke and Denis O'Conor. If those priests, clergymen and leaders of society had survived and continued in their ministries would the educational infrastructure of the diocese be expedited?

The religious orders, several of which lost members from fever, continued their efforts to alleviate the misery that surrounded them. Their building work resumed when, in 1848, the Franciscan school at Errew expanded to accommodate

500 pupils, cells for 20 monks, a commodious chapel with towers, offices and outhouses all by the indomitable perseverance of two or three devoted men, without money or means as a fund, within seven or eight years.

G.H. Moore MP donated thirty-two acres of land and MacHale gave £50 for the Franciscan monastery at Partry.[57] Granlahan monastery opened in 1853 on a site provided by the Lynch family of Lowberry. MacHale preached in Irish at the laying of the foundation stone for Cummer monastery in 1852.[58] Despite considerable efforts to substitute private enterprise for public grants the provision of schools was spasmodic. Franciscans Brothers and religious sisters in Tuam diocese struggled financially to conduct schools while their counterparts in other dioceses were permitted to accept national school grants. They were highly praised for their devotion to education and teacher training, but adequate funding remained a major obstacle. MacHale was unyielding in his quest for separate grants for schools along denominational lines. He was directly responsible for the creation of an educational vacuum in the diocese. The persons whom MacHale vilified were filling this vacuum.

The Protestant clergy and evangelists, through Bible societies, saw it as their duty to rescue Roman Catholics from 'the errors of Rome'. It was ironic that MacHale's own education policy was driving the children of his diocese into the Bible schools. Their perceived proselytism in the least literate parts of the archdiocese was widely publicised:

> There is a systematic attempt to seduce the Catholic poor of Ireland from their faith by means of bribery and intimidation. Money for this solicited from Protestants from all ranks; the greatest exertions are made to get Catholic children to attend Protestant schools. Appealed to the charity of Catholics throughout the world.[59]

Probably the most successful of the Bible societies was the Irish Church Missions to the Roman Catholics, the chief architect of which was the English clergyman, Alexander Dallas. The 1841 census of Ireland recorded that the least amount of education, in Ireland, was in the Protestant church union of Ballinakill in the west Galway area,[60] so he determined, unashamedly, to take advantage of its dreadful social conditions to further the Society's aims. He resolved to personally contact as many Roman Catholic homes in that area as possible. At the first sign of famine in 1845, the government issued a paper of inquiry concerning the state of crops in Ireland. Dallas grasped that opportunity to contact people, so his agents were engaged to distribute the papers of inquiry door-to-door, then post him the names and addresses so that he could compile a mailing list. On 16 January 1846 the 44,000 addressees received Protestant religious texts.[61] Within a few months, by mid 1846, private means for proselytising west Galway were in place.[62] The people had an avid desire for learning and schools were the most effective way of gaining their confidence. People power would yield a local network of schools. MacHale, cognizant of the fact that proselytism was rampant in the western parts of his diocese, in his Lenten pastoral of 1847

> deplored, that while many benevolent persons sympathise with the miseries of your poor flocks, there are to be found traders in fraud and fanaticism who wish to make merchandise of their souls. Of the cruel and inhuman schemes resorted to by these biblical traders the remote districts of this diocese afford lamentable evidence.[63]

Dallas visited Hyacinth D'Arcy's home at Clifden in 1848. A group of people awaited them at Errislannan to present an earnest petition signed by 163 persons living on the south side of Mannin Bay at Errismore:

> We are willing to submit to a course of education based on the scriptures, therefore your kindness to afford us such a facility for the improvement of our children shall be thankfully received and anxiously attended to, no matter what the opposition may be.

Soon 453 children attended his Errismore school. Some men from Clifden, however, attacked the master.[64] Dallas listened to many emissaries. He opened

3. Sellerna school house, *c.*1850

a school in an old storehouse at Sellerna where 150 children and 200 adults congregated on opening day. People were asked bilingually would they send their children to school if a new school was built, clearly understanding that it would mean leaving the 'false worship of Rome'.[65] Antagonism continued and in July 1848 the local priest was shouted at when he tried to induce the people to return to him by offering them some meal. Dallas persisted and, with the assistance of Protestant funds, the Irish Church Missions work continued and the first stone of the new school at Sellerna (fig. 3) was laid in October 1848.[66] With schools operating it was decided to formalise the arrangements of Dallas's missions, so the Irish Church Missions were formally formed by the end of 1848.[67] The animosity between the denominations intensified. This was open warfare, with all means, fair and foul, utilised to belittle and undermine the work of the opposition.

The commissioners, in 1831, were cautious in their approach to non-denominational schooling. One of their rules was that there was to be no connection between a national school and a place of worship. They could hardly have foreseen that twenty years later they would still have to maintain a delicate balance in resolving discord between the denominations. On 10 October 1851 E.I. Moore, the Protestant minister of Cong, wrote to the

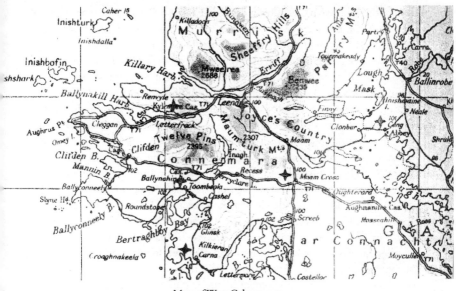

4. Map of West Galway area

commissioners 'will you kindly permit me to have an evening service in the national school room in Cornamona, distant about eight miles from my parish church'. A month later a reply was received – 'it is contrary to the rules that public worship should be celebrated in a national school'. Then Moore wrote that 'the priest has Mass there every second Sabbath. You must know about it from your inspector therefore you do not esteem Mass to be worship', to which the poor clerk in the commissioners' office in Marlborough Street replied 'we will lay your letter before the commissioner of education'. The commissioner advised the local inspector to 'put on a new padlock, and get police protection while so doing'.[68]

Bishop Plunket made ongoing Protestant funding available for the restructuring of the established church union of Ballinakill. He made an arrangement with the Ecclesiastical Commissioners by which the income of the deanery of Tuam (recently vacated) was applied to it.[69] The funding resulted in massive expansion.[70] In June 1852 an Irish Church Missions female training school was established at Clifden[71] before it was transferred to the central location of 19, Duke Street in Dublin the following October.[72] There was a growing demand for schools so money was urgently needed. Every Protestant clergyman was canvassed and urged to form a Ladies Association for fund raising. Funds, averaging about £20,000 a year, flowed in, but by the mid 1850s income was problematic and spasmodic. Dallas's friend Hyacinth D'Arcy was ordained by Thomas Plunket, bishop of Tuam and instituted next day to the living of Clifden.[73] Plunket rescued the mission when, in 1857, he established the West Connaught Church Endowment Society which became the chief funding agency of the Protestant mission in the western part of the diocese. By 1869 it endowed eleven churches at £150 annually.[74]

The resurgence of proselytism needed to be urgently addressed. MacHale and Plunket were both learned, stubborn, confident, arrogant, self-opinionated men and by 1850, as the country struggled with the aftermath of the Famine, the tide of episcopal opinion about the national schools was turning in their favour. The return of Paul Cullen from Rome in 1849, as successor to William Crolly, archbishop of Armagh, brought new Roman influence into the Irish church. MacHale must have felt vindicated by the pronouncement, at the 1850 Synod of Thurles, that denominational education was preferable to the national system. Ever optimistic, he hoped that after nearly twenty years of the system of national education, what he regarded as his voice of reason would be listened to. Cullen, meanwhile, very aware of the national schools impasse in MacHale's diocese, wrote to his successor Tobias Kirby, rector of the Irish College in Rome, on 28 October 1852: 'Proselytism continues in the west. People end up neither Protestant nor Catholic but infidel'.[75]

A policy of counter movement by the religious was escalated, but ongoing funding was a major problem. MacHale was consoled by the fact that –

> We have not been wanting, in union with the clergy and some of the enlightened laity in exertions to furnish the faithful with means of a sound Catholic education. Monasteries and convents established and now Christian Brothers' schools – though some want them to become national schools.[76]

He had not been found wanting, but his advisors were realists and recognised that education would penetrate into the four corners of the diocese only with government aid. MacHale was uncompromising in his pursuit of his own objectives. The commissioners appreciated the tremendous travail under which the religious toiled. MacHale continued to be very dogmatic when, in 1853, he forbade Dean Burke and the Sisters of Mercy at Westport to accept an unconditional annual grant of £100. Burke had been a candidate for the archbishopric twenty years earlier. As a man who worked diligently for the betterment of his people he had, in conjunction with the local landlord the marquess of Sligo initiated a national schools programme in Aughavale parish at Bouris, Kilmore, Mahastin, Kilsallagh, Clooneen, Drininduff, Midgefield, and Nappagh.[77] When MacHale voiced his opposition, he obeyed his directives, and all of these schools were closed. Many years of futile efforts, and quiet desperation, led him, as an older churchman, to confide in a very revealing letter to Kirby, in Rome, on 15 October 1853

> I can rest assured I was actuated solely by a sense of religion. Have often been pained at the apathy in the face of inroads on religion in the

diocese, especially in Achill, and regret I did not speak out long ago. I should have had the courage to establish national schools, which would have stopped the perversion. After the Synod of Thurles I felt impelled to do so hence the conflict. The continuous opposition of the archbishop to the national schools has had serious results. Proselytism in Achill and Connemara. The archbishop will not have schools unless there is a separate denominational grant to Catholics and Protestants. In fact the Catholics get nearly all the grant, and under a separate system the Protestants who have no need of it, would get more.[78]

Burke and many like-minded priests felt very aggrieved but following the suspension of Richard Gibbons in Castlebar they were silenced and painfully watched from the sidelines as Catholics in other dioceses benefited from education. Among Burke's curates was the newly ordained Bartholemew Cavanagh who was appointed to Westport in 1846. He is remembered, not as the manager of the schools in Knock parish, but as the parish priest at Knock at the time of the alleged apparition in 1879.[79]

In the years immediately following the great Famine the Sisters of Mercy responded to pleas for schools from larger parishes in the archdiocese. They embarked on an expensive programme of expansion into even the remotest parts of the archdiocese. At Westport and Tuam the Sisters had borne the brunt of the Famine and some of their members succumbed to the fever that enveloped so many. The Sisters' work of education and caring for the poor continued. In July 1854 they opened a school in Castlebar. On the twentieth anniversary of MacHale's elevation to the See of Tuam, 15 August 1854, an excellent breakfast and donations of clothes to the more destitute pupils, followed Mass in the convent chapel.[80] The good works of the Sisters continued when in 1860 MacHale donated £100 and laid the foundation stone for the Sisters of Mercy orphanage at Tuam.[81] Fundraising continued for the Sisters of Mercy elegant buildings overlooking the town of Clifden.[82] Designed by the well-known early Victorian architect John Sterling Butler,[83] they were opened in 1855. MacHale donated £1,400, and £300 came from Thomas Eyre of Bath[84] (he bought the D'Arcy estate at Clifden in the Encumbered Estate Courts). Other donations totaled £240.[85] By 1861, Clifden had two free schools,[86] one fee paying school with a total of 212 girls and a junior school for fifty boys who were under five years of age, and they all benefited from the attention of fifteen Sisters of Mercy. Thirty-five destitute orphans were 'fed, cared for and trained to be good servants.'[87] The Sisters of Mercy mission spread, and within a few years they commissioned architect John Joseph Lyons to prepare plans for a convent at Ballinrobe. The plans were costed at £3,000.[88] Again intensive fund raising continued and a charity sermon was preached at Gardiner Street Church in Dublin.[89] In 1855, in a substantial set-back to the progress of elementary education in other dioceses, the Royal Commission of Inquiry into primary education resolved that no clergyman of any denomination, or (except in the case of convent schools) member of any religious order, could be recognised as the teacher of a national school. Roman Catholic pressure grew stronger through the 1850s. Archbishop Daniel Murray of Dublin died in 1852 and Paul Cullen was transferred from Armagh to Dublin. Murray and Richard Whately, Protestant archbishop of Dublin, were commissioners for the previous twenty years. Cullen assumed power, decided not to accept the commissioner's post, and then felt free to attack the commissioners over the scripture content of some of the books sanctioned for use in national schools. Twenty years before that, Whately had compiled scripture extracts, which though sanctioned for use in schools, were not compulsory texts but were widely accepted. Cullen now questioned their use and Whately resigned amid much controversy. Now the Board of Education was bereft of two key figures who were most vocal adherents of denominational education – Murray and Whately. The balance they maintained for twenty years, as commissioners, was eroded. The national schools system entered a new phase in which clergy and teachers became a major force in the battle for an equitable system of popular elementary education.

Teacher development and local leadership

In 1861 the Board of National Education was thirty years old. The principled stand of the commissioners of national education in Ireland against denominational education had directly caused crises for Catholics and Protestants in the archdiocese of Tuam. The undermining of the social fabric through the post-Famine depletion and dissipation of the gentry, and through the persistent emigration of both major denominations, convinced many that their only future hope was to obtain an education for a life outside of Ireland. They were cognizant of the fact that the world opening up to them welcomed a literate, English-speaking work force. Postal and telegraphic communications and the advent of the railways revealed a window of opportunity. The dichotomy had denied a whole generation its basic right to education so the question needed to be earnestly revisited.

Elementary schools of one kind or another were dispersed throughout most parishes in the diocese of Tuam. The national schools inspectors had a herculean task, because, as the local face of the commissioners they had overall charge of national schools in their extensive school districts. When the Board was inaugurated eight inspectors were appointed to the prestigious posts at the massive annual salary of £300. In 1856 each received an annual salary of £125 and a horse, with a travel allowance of 5s. a day for each day on which he was obliged to travel to a greater distance than twenty miles from his residence.[1] In 1878 J.W. Greer schools inspector for Dunmore district, reported that

> During the year I examined 6,112 pupils for results in 106 schools, 5,665 pupils at secondary inspections. I made 142 incidental visits, and traveled 4,724 miles by car. As the average distance of my schools is sixteen miles from the centre, I spent on an average four hours daily in driving to and from the schools, in addition to five and a half hours per day in the actual inspection and examination of the schools.[2]

The commissioners saw it as their function to advance the use of the English language so it was the only language permitted in the national schools. The inspectors recognised the futility of this policy in the education of the monoglot Irish speaking population. In 1859 head inspector and later resident commissioner, Patrick J. Keenan proposed that in Irish-speaking districts children should be taught through the Irish language initially and afterwards one hour of Irish a day. This innovative proposal was ignored. Keenan wrote:

> It is hard to conceive any more difficult school exercise than to begin our first alphabet, and first syllabification, and first attempt at reading, in a language of which we know nothing, and all this without reference to, or comparison with our mother tongue.[3]

MacHale, a staunch lover of Irish, translated Moore's *Irish melodies*, six books of the *Iliad*, the *Pentateuch* (the first five books of the *Old Testament*), and Homer's first volume into Irish.

Denominational based education needed denominational educators. MacHale had forbidden his teachers to avail of training in the non-denominational Board of Education training college at Marlborough Street, Dublin. Teachers for Church Education Society schools trained at Kildare Place training college. The inspectors tried to improve teaching standards in national schools in Tuam diocese but basically the situation in the diocese had remained unchanged since the foundation of the Board of Education in 1831. The inspectors appreciated the contribution made to elementary education by the Franciscans at Errew and by the convents which, though not national schools, trained young teachers, who were then appointed to national schools. In most cases the principal teacher, generally untrained, was placed in charge of a school, had contact with the Board of Education, patron, managers and the local community, often at the tender age of seventeen or eighteen, without any education beyond fourth class. School registers, roll books, official timekeeping had all to be factored into a rigid timetable without any apprenticeship. All teachers were paid a flat rate salary of £8 per annum. This was counter-productive, so from 1839 the commissioners implemented a salary scale based on class. Promotion through the teacher-classes was on merit only. Ten years later, from 1849, all newly-appointed first-time national school teachers were probationers for at least a year until they passed the district inspector's Easter examination and were classed according to their competency. The report from James Patten, head inspector, on the state of teachers in Connacht in 1849,[4] showed that the number of trained, and the number of teachers in the higher classifications was very much lower in the Swinford and Westport areas than in other areas. Both districts are substantially within the archdiocese. The teachers were mainly deficient in reading, spelling and composition. The brighter senior pupils who assisted the teacher were paid a small salary and were known as monitors. Inspectors provided them, with a syllabus for four years of study to be supervised by the serving teacher. This presented problems, because only teachers who had no methodology and were barely literate had taught many of the older teachers. In 1861, the district inspector for Westport, Mr Macaulay, bemoaned the fact that in pre-national school times, it was claimed, 'the person on whom fell the lot of becoming a schoolmaster was some individual unfortunately maimed or decrepit, physically unable to work, and ashamed to beg – a pariah in society'.[5] As late as 1862 County Galway had hedge schools whose masters were generally very illiterate.[6] In the brave new world of national schools this type of person was certainly not a role model or one to whom the training of future teachers could be entrusted. Mr M'Sweeny, district inspector, Tuam:

> Of the 88 teachers employed in this district 40 per cent hold a rank below the first division of the third class, and I am of the opinion that this number, owing to a want of knowledge alone, are not competent to teach the course prescribed by the third programme, beyond the third class. There is only one remedy increase the staff of organising teachers.[7]

Teachers in Tuam archdiocese were plainly in need of a formal state-sanctioned, system of pre-service and in-service training. Mr Wilson, the district inspector for Galway wrote in 1862:

> From the beginning of the National Education system it was expected that teachers would be thoroughly educated. After thirty years of the system they were practically denied all access to books outside those on the Board's list.[8]

The blind adherence to rules sometimes went to ridiculous lengths as in the case of the teacher at Triehill national school who, instead of being commended on his initiative was, on 25 June 1861, reprimanded severely for having a newspaper in the classroom.[9] Teachers finally came together to improve their situation. The Irish Literary Teachers' Association was formed for the purpose of 'improving the condition of the teachers, both socially and intellectually, and rendering his position more permanent and more respected than it is at present.'[10]

The inspectors pleaded for some form of in-service training and in 1856 the commissioners appointed fifteen organising teachers. Organised school keeping was an art with which many of the school managers and teachers were only gradually becoming familiar. The inspectors promoted the assistance available from the organisers. They did not visit the schools in an autocratic mode but were there to help with discipline, teaching methods or organisation as they deemed essential:

> he is the living, speaking teachers' manual – the model, competent to instruct by his example alone, in establishing a proper sense of discipline. I am of opinion that taking into account the wants and the

circumstances of the national system at present, that the managers should understand that the organizers would be employed to improve the system of teaching in their schools without requiring any support on their part; and that they should be directed to visit such schools as the inspectors should select, but such selection should be subject to the approval of the Board.[11]

Applications for grants began to trickle in to the commissioners from parishes where national schools had been closed over twenty years earlier. It was indeed a move to be welcomed. The local contribution presented a stumbling block in impoverished parishes. The schools had to be built to plans and specifications as supplied by the Board of Works.

Table 4. Grants for the erection of schoolhouses, 1864

Number of children to be accommodated	Total estimated cost, including school furniture and out-offices		Board of Education grant		Description of school
	£	s	£	s	
60	207		138		Single school room
75	225		150		Single school room
100	255		170		Single school room
120	306		204		Single school room
150	416	5	277	10	Two rooms on ground
150	360		240		Two rooms, one over the other
200	487	10	325		Two rooms on ground
200	435		290		Two rooms, one over the other

Source: Papers relating to national education, Ireland, HC 1864 (157), xlvi, 346.

By 1862 there were 162 national schools with 14,700 pupils in the Tuam archdiocese. 98 per cent of the pupils and 99 per cent of the 297 teachers were Roman Catholics. 25 per cent of the national schools were under Established Church patrons and catered for 200 Protestant and 4,000 Catholic pupils. In the absence of local Catholic or national schools many Catholic pupils attended the Irish Church Missions and Church Education Society's schools. Catholic parents were determined to access free education for their children even though the ethos of the national schools, and particularly national schools under Protestant patronage, was anathema to MacHale. Non-Catholic parents were equally anxious to educate their children, so about 100 of their children attended national schools under Catholic patrons.[12]

The persistent criticisms of the inspectors about the ineptitude of teachers, due to their lack of methodology, were noted. Allegations about the non-denominational stance of the model schools persisted. Pressure was brought to bear on the commissioners when, in 1863, the bishops decreed that no Catholics were to attend the model schools. Furthermore, any teacher who trained in a model school, after the ban took effect, would not be employed by any priest or by his consent in any national school. In 1860 the *Catholic Directory* reported that MacHale was considering establishing a training school for teachers. In November 1863 the Board of Education decided to allow formal training of teachers at any school in the national schools system which the inspectors assessed as being competent to train teachers. This prompted the Sisters of Mercy in Baggot Street Dublin, who had conducted a teacher-training institution for several years, to apply for official recognition from the Board. Despite the avowed policy of expanding teacher-training opportunities the commissioners replied, on 4 January 1864, that it was entirely out of their power to comply with that request.[13] Twenty years were to elapse before MacHale's plea was addressed with the establishment of denominational teacher training colleges.

Patrick Weston Joyce, one of the organising teachers, saw the acute need for, diligently compiled and, in February 1863, published the first of seventeen editions of *A handbook of school management and methods of teaching, a textbook for national teachers*. It set out in great detail all the steps that needed to be considered from the first discussion on the provision of a national school to the actual reception of scholars; and the best methods of ensuring that scholar's steady progress through the school. It dealt with the selection of a site; the plans and costs of building and fitting up the school. It went on to the selection of teachers and monitors and their professional development; then practical school organisation; and gave guidance on child psychology and teaching methods. School keeping, as exemplified by Joyce, was as important as academic achievements. He did not deal with moral or religious education. It was altogether a very practical basic handbook for the patron, manager and staff. The manual had its uses, but it was only an aid to the more literate teacher and of very limited assistance to the poorly educated teachers. Mr M'Sweeney, the inspector for Tuam district, obviously fearful that a handbook might be over-relied upon, or be regarded as an alternative to a properly structured course of training wrote:

> Much has been said about the want of teachers' manuals in the national schools to direct them in the art of intelligent and effectual teaching, but such a manual would no more accomplish such an end than a manual on drawing would make them teachers of art.[14]

Joyce developed a career in the forefront of education as a writer, a historian and, from 1883, professor of Irish at the training college.

In 1859, and again in January 1866, the Roman Catholic bishops appealed to the government. In 1859, following much agitation and discussion, the Board of Education became pro-Catholic with the appointment as commissioners of ten Catholics and ten Protestants. The Catholics had a working majority among the commissioners because they were able to act as a unit while the Protestant commissioners often split among themselves. The government was satisfied that the visionary scheme of national education had proved eminently successful. They believed that the rules of the Board not only protected the minority from being oppressed, but also the majority from being the oppressors. In 1866, the Roman Catholic bishops petitioned Home Secretary Sir George Grey that all Catholic schools, which were attended exclusively by Catholics, should become strictly denominational and that all model schools should cease. Grey, on behalf of the government, supported the status quo, and stated that the system of national education 'is well adapted to the peculiar circumstances of Ireland' and 'has been the means of conferring very great advantages on this country and the commissioners would regard with sincere regret any step tending to its overthrow'.[15] The bishops were not intent on its overthrow but on accepting the situation as it had evolved where most schools were in fact denominational. The government ordered a full investigation of the system.

In 1868 the Royal Commission on Primary Education in Ireland (better known as the Powis Commission from the name of its chairman, the earl of Powis), proceeded to examine the system of national education and other agencies providing education for the poor.[16] The Protestant Church Education Society defended its policy of combined religious and secular education and explained why it found it impossible to accept aid from the national board (with its policy of separate religious and literary instruction). For the first time in the life of the national schools system the Roman Catholic bishops and teachers were given a fair hearing. One of the outcomes of the commission's deliberations, which must have vindicated MacHale, was the recognition of the right of the Protestants and Roman Catholics to denominational schools. The distinction between Roman Catholic religious schools and ordinary national schools should cease. MacHale was hailed as a hero and champion of education. Denominational national schools had been achieved but they were, however, still governed by the original rules for national schools that forbade combined literary and secular instruction.

At this time, in 1870, MacHale, despite having reached almost four score years, went to Rome to attend the first Vatican Council. While at the Vatican he met Fermanagh-born bishop John Joseph Lynch of Toronto who was elevated to archbishop while in Rome. In 1860, when Lynch was elevated to the See of Toronto he inherited a system of publicly financed non-denominational schools. In 1865 he was instrumental in gaining a denominational system of education and from 1867 he sought improved conditions for these public schools.[17] In an astute reading of the political realities he had accepted government grants for schools while continuing his quest for his type of schools. MacHale consulted him, and was apparently influenced by him, about the newly established commission on education. In any event, the Powis Commission recommended denominational schools. MacHale had achieved his objective but under the Board's terms of separate literary and religious instruction. For this reason it was only after MacHale's death, in 1881, that the Franciscan monastery schools and the convent schools in the diocese joined the national schools system. In a friendship which spanned the next decade Lynch and MacHale witnessed the British government accede to many of the educational requests, which had been debated so vigorously but denied, over the previous forty years.

Teachers were totally beholden to the commissioners and to the schools' management. They had no security of tenure, accommodation adjacent to their schools was often problematic, and the difficulty of providing for an insecure future was enormous. From the mid 1850s, they believed that by joining together they might be listened to just as the clergy's demands were being recognised. They formed local teachers' associations in the belief that unity is strength and that as individual teachers they were virtually powerless against all the forces of authority. A meeting of the national teachers in Strabane district on 5 October 1867 decided to invite members of other teachers' groups to Strabane. On 26 October the chairman P. McGowan welcomed the national teachers. C. Matthew's minutes noted that 'it is in no spirit of restlessness, no morbid striving after notoriety; no undue estimation of their own importance, that has forced the quiet, retiring, practical national teachers into this association.' They resolved 'we demand, for properly qualified teachers, a more independent position in national schools; and emoluments that will help them to maintain a state in society suitable to their office and the extent of their attainments.'[18]

Archbishop MacHale was in his mid-seventies when the teachers of Ireland initiated the cohesiveness, absent during the earlier years of national education, and through his more forceful years. The teachers in Tuam diocese welcomed, in 1868, the formation of the Irish National Teachers' Association – later the Irish National Teacher's Organisation. This organisation of teachers at grass-roots level set the pace for the amelioration of their grievances, and in the next decade accomplished more in raising their professional status, than had been achieved in the previous half a century. In 1868 seventy-one of the teachers' associations throughout the country came together as the Irish National Teachers' Association, under the presidency of Vere Foster, a wealthy member of a County Louth landed family. He was convinced that a practical business-like approach towards improving the conditions of pupils and teachers should be adopted by a united, well-qualified and adequately remunerated body of teachers. Foster, who died in December 1900, is best remembered as the designer of headline copies that sold for 1*d*. or ½*d*.

according to the quality of the paper. They were 'good enough for the richest – cheap enough for the poorest'.[19] An enterprising Dublin publisher, Albert E. Chamney launched the *Irish Teachers' Journal* on 1 January 1868. His stated aim was that the journal would be

> a monthly record of educational movement and a medium of discussion, interchange, and correspondence for Irish schoolmasters and teachers. Teachers of all classes and creed may peruse its pages with equal pleasure and profit.[20]

The *Journal* published government education policy; advocated improvement of teachers' social status and invited contributions from practical teachers'. The *Irish Teachers' Journal* continued until the Irish National Teacher's Organisation began publishing the *Irish School Weekly*, in 1904. Teachers saw their *Journal* as a very welcome and useful medium of exchange. The *Journal*, in its first issue, provided detailed instruction on how to form a teachers' club: 'appoint a secretary to call a small initial meeting; at the meeting pass resolution to form a teachers' association; secretary to forward to each teacher within a certain radius a copy of the resolution, together with an invitation to join; call a general meeting and lay rules for association before the meeting; invite paper to be read at next meeting; collect small sum as entrance fee to meet contingencies; twenty to thirty teachers in each association; central association in Dublin to receive money from each association; then let the work begin in earnest at once.' The *Journal* continued: 'One man thoroughly in earnest is worth a dozen indifferent or lethargic helpmates'.[21]

The commissioners faced teacher-power when on the 15 August 1874, 1000 (900 male and 100 female) representatives of teachers met in the Rotunda in Dublin. The Tuam archdiocesan associations sent an all-male representation – John McCarrick, Ballyglass (Castlebar), Morrin (Newport), Egan (Central Mayo), Falloon and Kenny (Westport) and Beirne (Mountbellew).[22] An early secretary of the all Ireland Irish National Teacher's Organisation was John Morrin, who accompanied delegations to the Board of Education and to the government in London. One by one the teachers' representatives pursued the recommendations of the Powis Commission. Reports began to trickle in from the new associations, with Finnegan of Athlone and Donaghy of Mount Temple mentioned in the first report to be published, which came from Moate, County Westmeath. Teachers within the Tuam archdiocese were quick to become actively involved in forming teachers' clubs. Teachers such as John Morrin, John Carabine of Williamstown agricultural school and John Egan, Burriscarra national school were aware of the potential salary and status of teachers from their time in Marlborough Street training college. They regarded MacHale's outmoded attitude as a barrier to the advancement of education. Carabine was the organiser of the Glenamaddy Teachers' Association that claimed to be a Mutual Improvement Society with the view of raising the professional status of junior members.[23] Egan, Associate in Arts (First Class), formerly a professor at St Malachy's College in Belfast, responded to the need for educating his less fortunate colleagues by providing teaching guidance through the pages of the *Journal*.

Teaching was not seen as the best and most attractive career for the more entrepreneurial young man in the archdiocese. In parishes without national schools the hedge schools still persisted. The commissioners and the inspectors recognised the need for teacher training and the inadequacy of the teachers' salary, initially paid on a half-yearly basis.

Table 5. Scale in force for the payment of salaries to teachers, 1832–80

	Males							Females						
Class	1st			2nd		3rd		1st			2nd		3rd	
Division of class	1st	2nd	3rd	1st	2nd	1st	2nd	1st	2nd	3rd	1st	2nd	1st	2nd
Period	£	£	£	£	£	£	£	£	£	£	£	£	£	£
1832–1839	–	–	–	–	–	–	10	–	–	–	–	–	–	10
1839–1848	20	–	–	15	–	12	–	15	–	–	12	–	10	–
1848–1849	30	25	22	20	18	16	14	24	20	18	15	14	13	12
1849–1851	30	25	22	21	19	17	15	24	20	18	16	15	14	13
1851–1852	35	28	24	21	19	17	15	24	20	18	16	15	14	13
1852–1855	36	30	25	22	20	18	15	25	22	19	17	16	15	13
1855–1859	46	38	32	26	24	20	17	36	30	24	22	20	17	15
1859–1860	50	42	36	30	26	22	18	40	34	28	24	22	18	16
1860–1872	52	44	38	32	28	24	18	42	36	30	26	22	20	16
1872–1875	52	38	–	30	30	24	24	42	30	–	24	24	20	20
1875–1880	58	44	–	38	38	32	32	48	36	–	30	30	25	25
1880–	70	53	–	44	44	35	35	58	43	–	35	35	28	28

Source: *Forty-seventh report CNEI*, Appendix O, H.C. 1881 [C.2925–1], xxxiv, 516.

The pay structure tried to encourage a better class of applicant but MacHale's embargo on training kept the teachers in subjugation. Mr Macaulay, Westport district inspector reported:

> teachers have become a respectable body of men. Their social standing is a fictitious one, because their inadequate pay will not support a family, and enable a teacher to dress or appear in public as should a man who aspires to be considered superior to his neighbours; and his neighbours are shrewd enough to observe how the physical comforts are sacrificed to appearances.[24]

Table 6. Results fees for National School Teachers, 1878

Subjects	Infants		First		Second		Third		Fourth		Fifth		Fifth		Sixth		Sixth	
	s	d	s	d	s	d	s	d	s	d	s	d	s	d	s	d	s	d
Reading			2	0	2	0	2	6	2	6	2	6	2	6	2	6	2	6
Spelling			1	0	1	0	1	0	1	0	1	0	1	0	1	0	1	0
Writing			1	0	1	0	1	6	1	6	1	6	1	6	2	0	2	0
Arithmetic			1	0	2	0	2	6	2	6	2	6	2	6	3	0	3	0
Grammar							0	6	1	0	1	6	1	6	1	6	1	6
Geography					1	0	1	0	1	6	1	6	1	6	1	6		
Agriculture									2	0	2	6	2	6	3	0	3	0
Book-keeping											2	6	2	6	3	0	3	0
Needlework					0	6	1	0	2	0	2	6	2	6	3	0	3	0
Maximum value, male national schools:	3	0	5	0	6	6	9	0	11	6	15	6	15	6	17	6	17	6
Maximum value, female national schools:	3	0	5	0	6	6	10	0	11	6	15	6	15	6	17	6	17	6
Extras (inside or out of school hours):																		
Singing			1	6	1	6	2	6	2	6	2	6	3	0	3	0		
Drawing					2	6	2	6	2	6	2	6	3	0	3	0		
Other approved extra subjects (each):											5	0	5	0	5	0	5	0
Classics (out of school hours):																		
Greek											10	0	10	0	10	0	10	0
Latin											10	0	10	0	10	0	10	0
French											5	0	5	0	5	0	5	0

Source: C.N.E.I., *Forty-fourth report, 1877*, Appendix A, HC 1878–79 [2223], xxiv, 102.

Salaries were issued quarterly from 1 April 1850, with the reminder that hopefully it would be paid within three weeks from the period from which it became due. The salary of the average classed principal teacher in Ireland did not exceed £14. 10s. per annum even though the salary scale was from £13 to £30. Assistant teachers and probationers were paid £9 or £10 (table 5).[25] These inadequate salaries persisted. Teachers were not only poorly paid but they were a much maligned group of people who had severe punishment meted out to them for unbecoming conduct or infringement of the school rules. One teacher was fined the exorbitant sum of 10s. – possibly two weeks salary – for closing the school before the appointed hour on 25 May 1859.[26] The *Irish Teachers' Journal*, in its first edition, 1 January 1868, revealed that Irish schoolmasters are in Canada, USA – teaching, trading, lumbering, driving, or cultivating; in Australia and New Zealand gold-digging, sheep-tending, farming or trading – abroad as a sailor – abroad anywhere – being anything, doing anything that will give him the living and the hope denied at home'. It concluded 'the teacher is abroad because he is starved at home.' It continued 'the National Board does not, perhaps cannot, allow to the highest class of its teachers – men who have to stand an examination that would bother a bishop – and leave a cabinet minister dumb-founded – the wages of a carpenter. True they get something besides a salary; but that something is very often a slight improvement on nothing.' Part of the teachers' remuneration came by payments from the parents and guardians of their pupils. It was an insecure form of remuneration but Mr Seymour, district inspector, Westport reported, in 1864, 'The people have the wit never to pay a bad teacher'.[27] The fees effectively debarred some families or members of families from the schools.

The Irish National Teachers' Organisation reviewed salary scales and in order to attract better teachers and to encourage education parliament was petitioned. In 1876 it raised teachers' salaries by a complex and circuitous route, by implementing the Powis Commission's payment by results system (table 6). The government would pay one third of the salary, another third would be paid for results, if a matching third came from local sources.

In order to be eligible to be examined for results a pupil needed to have attended school for at least 100 days that year. The teacher was given a fee for each basic subject that each pupil passed, and received the payment as an annual lump sum. Teachers were against the results system from the very beginning as school attendance was not compulsory until 1892. An assistant teacher could not be appointed until the average attendance reached seventy pupils. The system did not allow for less able pupils. However, parliament decided in the National School Teachers (Ireland) Act in 1875 that it would pay one-third on condition that the final third was provided locally as had always been the case. Now, however, instead of individual families paying fees the salary supplement would be levied on the local rates and paid over to the teachers by the local board of guardians; but they rightly saw the education of the poor as a central government responsibility. They convened meetings to discuss avoiding the new levy on the local rates. Over the next year the *Irish Teachers' Journal* reported that all the boards of guardians in the archdiocese declined to become contributory unions. The teachers were disturbed by the refusal and one very disgruntled P.K. McGovern of Tarmon National School, secretary of Castlerea Teachers' Association, wrote that Castlerea Union met under the chairmanship of a local landlord, Mr Wills Sandford. The local MP, Charles Owen O'Conor of Clonalis House Castlerea, spoke in favour of the union contributing. However the other members did not agree,[28] and so the teachers in north County Galway and Ballinlough in County Roscommon were denied part of their result fees. In common with many other teachers McGovern was understandably crestfallen when he wrote:

> the motion was supported by the ability, wealth, intelligence of the Board but the plebian and illiterate elements prevailing, avarice, ignorance and parsimony were destined for a time to triumph over the cause of liberality, progress and education.[29]

It is reasonable to expect that the remuneration of teachers along the western seaboard would be fairly similar. The following figure shows the wide disparities.

Table 7. Income of national teachers, 1873

	No of teachers	average salary p.a.	Results fee	Total
County Galway	341	£35. 7s.	£6	£41. 7s.
County Mayo	401	£35. 9s.	£6. 4s.	£41. 13s.
County Clare	321	£43. 13s.	£8. 8s.	£52. 1s.

Source: Irish Teachers' Journal, 18 May 1874.

In County Clare, mainly in the diocese of Killaloe, an average teacher was taking home about 25 per cent more money than a teacher in either of the other two counties. Counties Galway and Mayo are divided into several different dioceses. Salary figures are not available on a diocesan basis but it is quite likely that teachers in Tuam archdiocese received up to 40 per cent less than their County Clare counterparts. The payment by results figure in these three counties is very interesting – the higher the average salary of the teacher the higher the results fee.

One of the early concessions was to teachers who, until 1872, had no security of tenure. Then the board decided that it would withdraw support from any school manager who refused to have a contract of employment with a teacher with a three months termination clause on either side. Another long-held grievance of teachers was the difficulty of accumulating savings to enable them to secure themselves financially in their senior years. Thirty years had passed since 1846 when the commissioners advocated to parliament the propriety of extending to Ireland an arrangement for giving retiring pensions to old and meritorious teachers. They reported 'we have ascertained that the plan in question is under consideration though not fully matured'.[30] Pensions had been discussed, promised and promptly forgotten. The Irish National Teachers' Organisation responded with horror to the shocking revelation in the 1871 census that there were 111 former teachers living in workhouses.[31] Prospects were improved when a contributory pension fund was granted from 1879, when funds were released as a consequence of disestablishment of the Church of Ireland under the Irish Church Act of 1869.[32]

The Irish National Teachers' Organisation urgent call for residences for teachers resulted, in 1875, in the provision of grants for teachers' residences. One of the conditions attached to the government grants for residences was the same as grants for schools in that one-third of the cost had to be raised locally.[33] It was a vicious circle – poor living accommodation – low classification

– low salary – poor living accommodation. Vere Foster again came to the rescue of the teachers with his system of grants of £50 each as the local contribution to access the government grant.[34] Many teachers in the arch-diocese owed a debt of gratitude to Foster as they enjoyed a superior standard of accommodation in their residences – usually built adjacent to, but not on, school grounds. Teachers by joining together had, by 1878, achieved security of tenure, improved remuneration and access to grants towards living accommodation. They were very actively involved in what was an all-Ireland teachers' movement.

The formation of the Irish National Teachers' Organisation and the publication of the *Irish Teachers' Journal* proved a catalyst to professional development opportunities which were widely welcomed. From the very beginning of the Irish National Teachers' Organisation, lectures by experienced and well-regarded teachers, such as Simon Comer's talk on *Arithmetic* and John Carabine's lecture on *Reading*, at Glenamaddy were well attended.[35] Many of the teachers were native Irish speakers but they were ill equipped to formally teach the language. The Irish National Teachers' Organisation empowered its members to seek, even after a lifetime, the educationally desirable use of the vernacular for teaching purposes. Teachers, unsure of their right to congregate for Irish studies, decided to meet simultaneously, on the second Saturday in September 1868, at Castlebar, Claremorris and Ballinrobe to study the *Phonic method of teaching elementary Gaelic*.[36] The *Irish Teachers' Journal* published a series entitled *Lessons in the Irish language* in 1874. Ten years later Edmond Dowling, district inspector in Galway bemoaned the fact:

> that children come to school not very young, up to nine years of age, and yet unable to speak one word of English and with an exceedingly meagre Irish vocabulary. Teachers in the Irish speaking localities, although able to speak Irish, do not, with two exceptions know it as a written language.[37]

In 1877 a memorial was sent to the Chief Secretary urging the recognition of Irish as an extra subject in schools. The fairly worthless concession was made that, from 1879, the scholars could be taught, as an extra subject, on the payment of an extra school fee. This, small but significant step by the commissioners was welcomed by the local teachers.[38] The greatest demand should come from the Irish speaking districts in the west, but due to poverty the fees were not forthcoming, so the subject was not submitted for examination. After five years the fees for learning Irish were abolished by the Treasury. There was a very poor demand for an Irish language headline copy-book on the commissioners list of books. With the advent of teacher training colleges, the Society for the preservation of the Irish language sought to have the Irish language accepted as a subject in the examination for first-class teachers. At the Irish National Teachers' Organisation's congress, in 1882, it was stated that to have Irish as a subject in teacher training colleges would cost the Board of Education no more than £300 a year. The Board acceded to their request, but only three teachers presented for the examination.

While the teachers were educating themselves they were concerned about their fellow adults who did not complete a formal education. The average national school pupil had finished his schooling when he had passed through third or fourth class. Many pupils did not come to school until they were strong enough to walk perhaps two or three miles each way. To cope with the demand for further education evening national schools were established in some areas as at Tubberoe, Kilconla, which had one of the first national schools, and was established under the patronage of the Protestant Lynch family.[39] The extras most commonly taught were algebra and geometry.[40] Michael Kenny, a former seminarian at Maynooth College and later principal at Carrick national school Ballinlough taught Latin and Greek as extra subjects in the evening. Among the books studied were Cicero, Virgil, Homer and Livy.[41] His assistant Michael Mannion taught reading, writing and arithmetic on three evenings a week from 6 p.m. to 9 p.m. Twenty-seven male adults with an average age of twenty-one attended. The fee was 3*d*. per week.[42]

People in the archdiocese of Tuam could see a future in which, ironically, a good education would be a necessary requisite for emigrants 'as a means of getting a situation'. In October 1879 Michael Davitt started the Land League in Castlebar. The three demands of the Land League were fair rent, to be assessed by arbitration; fixity of tenure, while the rent was paid; freedom for the tenant to sell his right of occupancy for the best market price. People did not regard education with a view to the improvement of the yield of agriculture, indigenous manufacturing industries or the trade of the country. There was a great demand for skilled trades people and the dearth of them impeded the school-building programme. People who emigrated to America sent home reports of a land of full employment. The number of Irish-born persons actually living in the USA almost doubled in the years 1850–90 from 962,000 to 1,872,000.[43] Emigrant remittances were welcomed but it was not until 1882–4 that the British government provided state-aided passages. Archbishop Lynch, MacHale's friend, visited the west of Ireland shortly before MacHale's death.[44] Lynch was among the bishops who invited priests to accompany and minister to the emigrants. In a gesture of solidarity MacHale bequeathed him the chasuble, dalmatian and tunic which Pope Pius VIIII bestowed on him fifty years earlier.[45] In parts of the archdiocese priests opposed the emigration plans, but Patrick Levingstone, curate and founder, in 1888, of six national schools at Williamstown, accompanied his people and ministered for several years at Albany in New York state.[46]

MacHale's demonising of the national school system served only to promote his public persona. He received much adulation on his high profile trips to Rome and then by coach to Paris (where his nephew Thomas was

Table 8. National Schools, Tuam archdiocese, which received
grant approval, 1880–87

Parish	Schools
Abbey knockmoy	Crumlin.
Achill	Tonragee
Aglish	Derrylea, St Joseph's, Aglish, St Bridget's, St Patrick's, St Mary's.
Annagh	Coolnafarna.
Aran	Creggakireen, Innismaan, Inniseer, Killeany.
Ballindoon	Aillebrack, Calla,.
Ballinrobe	Cregduff, Cloonlifeen, Roxborough, Treen, Ballinrobe convent.
Ballintubber	Derreendaiderg.
Ballynakill	Clifden, Beylick, Clifden convent. Tully.
Bekan	Ballinvilla, Brackloon.
Burrishoole	Knockaloughra, Lettermoghera, Cushlecka, Convent, Rossgalive.
Claremorris	Meelickmore, Garryedmond, Loughanamon, Birchfield.
Clonberne	Mahanagh
Crossboyne	Carrowsteelaun, Seefin.
Cummer	Cummer.
Donoghpatrick	Caherlistrane
Dunmore	Shanballymore, Gortnaleam, Garrafrauns, Dunmore.
Drum	Lough Mask.
Kilcommon	Gortskehi, Lehinch.
Kildacommogue	Keelogues
Kilgeever	Clare island, Inishturk.
Kilkerrin	Kilkerrin
Killererin	Garra.
Killerursa	Kilcoona, Inishmacateer.
Kilmaine	Kilmaine
Kilmeena	Culleenmore, Myna.
Kilmolara	Neale.
Lackagh	Lackagh
Liskeevy	Belmont, Milltown, Dalgin.
Moylough	Mount Bellew.
Moyrus	Feenish island, Carna, Lettermullan, Carna convent, Mynish island, Moyrus, Loughconeerra.
Omey	Dunloughan, Kingstown, Aughris, Aughrismore, Clifden, Omey island.
Partry	Treen, Killetaine.
Robeen	Ballygarries.
Ross	Finney, Shanafarahan, Kilmilkin, Cluinbroon.
Turlough	Greenans, Caurane, Park.
Westport	Killavalla.
Williamstown	Leatra, Polredmond, Ballyroe.

rector of the Irish College). On his peregrinations through England, he preached well-received and handsomely productive charity sermons for his schools and churches, as he journeyed from the south coast through London, to embark for Dublin at Liverpool. After one such trip, on his return to Dublin, in 1870, from the Vatican Council he was hailed as a hero at Coffey's Hotel in Dominick Street in Dublin when twenty-five bands assembled to play 'God save Ireland'. A green flag with an Irish harp was hoisted in his honour.[47] At Tuam he was ceremoniously accompanied through gaily-decorated streets from the railway station to his palace. One hundred guests attended a dinner in his honour where speeches referred 'in gladsome strains to his unsurpassing qualities and talents, his patriotism and personal worth.'[48] He was a personal and honoured friend of more than one of the popes, six of whom he had seen elected at Rome. In 1875, on the occasion of the golden jubilee of his elevation to the episcopacy a marble statue was unveiled to him in Tuam. The sculpture by Thomas Farrell, a prominent sculptor of the period, was erected in front of his cathedral of St Jarlath in which he had taken a great pride. MacHale's last public appearance in Dublin was as chairman on the occasion of the unveiling of a statue of his friend, the late Sir John Gray, with whom he had maintained a strong friendship. Gray was the former owner of the *Freeman's Journal* and a Liberal MP who had espoused several causes alongside MacHale. In 1881, MacHale was the oldest prelate of the Roman Catholic church in the world.

In 1879 John MacEvilly, bishop of Galway, and former president of St Jarlath's college in Tuam was appointed as his coadjutor with rights of succession. An acrimonious relationship ensued. MacEvilly had established a vibrant system of national schools in Galway diocese. Within a few years of MacHale's death in 1881, MacEvilly undertook a programme of refurbishment and rebuilding established schools and providing new ones (table 8).

Schools were now in every parish but school attendance remained spasmodic. In 1892 the Irish Education Act made education compulsory for children between the ages of six and fourteen, but in order to make the compulsion element more acceptable some modifications were conceded. An eleven-year-old pupil who completed the programme for fourth class was considered to be adequately educated and was no longer compelled to attend school. In the days of non-existent transport facilities another clause was inserted in the Act whereby country pupils living more than two miles from the nearest school were not obliged to attend.

Conclusion

The landscape of the archdiocese of Tuam, in the nineteenth century, was transformed by the development of a road, rail and waterways network. A booming population and recurrent famines turned the eyes of many to the opportunities offered by America and the great industrial centers of Britain. Emigration and the development of the post and telegraph services made people receptive to a literate world. For the first time in the history of Ireland, the acquisition of literacy and the English language, was a major ambition of the poor in the west of Ireland.

John MacHale, as archbishop of Tuam, was central to the story of elementary education in Ireland from his elevation to the see of Tuam in 1834 until his death in 1881. He was the first alumnus of St Patrick's College, Maynooth to be elected bishop. In that assertive self-confident phase in Catholicism in Ireland, he obviously saw himself as the standard-bearer in future relations between the Irish Roman Catholic episcopacy and the government; and he set out to foster good personal relationships with the popes and Propaganda Fide. Catholic Emancipation was a very live issue in parliament; and the long-running inquiries into what parliament perceived as the optimum strategy for the elementary education of Ireland's poor were concluding with the adoption of the system of national education. MacHale saw himself as a proactive clerical gentleman and businessman, who by pursuing ideological objectives openly and vigorously, would hasten a denominational school system.

Power Le Poer Trench (the last in a long line of Protestant archbishops of Tuam), and his successor Thomas Plunket, (first bishop of the united diocese of Tuam, Killala and Achonry), with their wealthy family connections, were in a financial position to remain outside of the national schools system for the first forty years. An educated, emerging Roman Catholic people and a diminishing number of Protestants led to the disestablishment of their church, and the gradual integration of their schools and scholars into the national schools system.

The legacy of Alexander Dallas, the English clergyman who, in 1848, founded the Irish Church Missions to the Roman Catholics was a network of schools in the most westerly part of the diocese. Those schools were opened in a blaze of animosity and with the backing of English philanthropists. Were it not for the adoption of Irish Church Missions schools by Plunket, as bishop, funding fatigue would have hastened their demise. They declined gradually and the remainder were subsumed into the national schools system.

Archbishop MacHale inherited, in 1834, a diocese in crisis. Its church-going population was less than half the number of nominal Roman Catholics. The people were in a pessimistic mood, with their disintegrating woolen and linen cottage industries, due to the rapid growth in cheaper, mass-produced materials in the industrial cities of Britain. Population was spiraling out of control. The uncertainty surrounding cholera and typhus diseases, with the complete lack of medical care, rendered the people helpless. Education for the poor was given with the connivance of the landlord and, indeed, often in secret, in dismal surroundings. The parents of the scholars had, in their youth, been denied Roman Catholic schoolmasters and the aim of all state-funded schools was to proselytise. Then news began to filter through of a state-sponsored national schools system with separate literary and religious instruction. It was welcomed by the Roman Catholic episcopacy, as a system that if monitored, would achieve the end result of a literate people.

MacHale saw dangers to the faith of his people lurking within the rules for national schools. Roman Catholicism should embrace the whole person and could not be compartmentalised into separate religious and literary instruction. Even Propaganda did not altogether agree with his interpretation of the ethos of the national schools. MacHale clearly saw himself as the ruling authority on education for his people. The fact that there are no personal papers available from MacHale (other than the edited papers in Bernard O'Reilly's book) raises the question of whom, or how widely, did MacHale consult before he made that fateful announcement at Castlebar chapel in 1840. His friend, the highly respected and influential rector of the Irish College in Rome, Paul Cullen, nor his senior parish priests Richard Gibbons of Castlebar and Bernard Burke of Westport did not agree with his conclusions. Many of the priests suffered grave crises of conscience in following MacHale's dictates. Teachers were left with the choice of hedge school conditions or the emigrant ship. Parents, pupils and whole communities were robbed of their only chance of a well-regulated system of education.

The fact that MacHale was an arrogant, self-opinionated man can be in no doubt. Did the Famine of the 1840s leave him devoid of some of his confidants such as Loftus and O'Regan? Did the enormous post-Famine financial diffi-culties, which burdened many of his wealthy gentry and merchant friends, lead him into a state of confusion and inactivity? During the Famine he had been instrumental in the raising and distribution of vital funds. He had pleaded for and accepted help from the British government; yet he had spurned all assistance towards an education which would have helped his people to a life independent of the vagaries of the weather on their food supply. We can only conjecture that MacHale misjudged the mood of the government. National schools were available. It was a question of accepting them in their entirety or doing without. They could not, and would not, be altered to suit one individual – even an individual as powerful as MacHale perceived himself to be.

The development of the status of teachers, from illiterate hedge schoolmasters to a body of respected professional educators, took more than a lifetime. Here again MacHale's dominance is evident, in that he would not countenance any teacher training, except the most ad hoc kind provided by the monasteries and convents. Members of his own family circle were not excluded from educational opportunities as his nephew Thomas became rector of the Irish College in Paris, his nephew Richard parish priest of Claremorris and another nephew was a solicitor.

The attitudes of the British government began to change slightly in the 1860s. The reorganisation of the Board of Education to include a 50 per cent Roman Catholic group of commissioners led to a heightened awareness of the necessity of some concessions to the Roman Catholic majority. This change would probably have come about for demographic reasons but MacHale regarded it a vindication of his life-long stance on denominational education.

The formation of the Irish National Teachers' Organisation, in 1868, was the major turning point in the educational life of the diocese. It brought teachers together in the towns and villages and, through their united efforts, they formed well-motivated groups, to enhance the future possibilities of both themselves and their pupils. Their influence became so powerful that, in 1894, the INTO was proscribed in both Tuam and Armagh diocese, under the terms of the Maynooth statutes. The clergy, once again, held the upper hand. MacHale hindered the advancement of his people over half a century. In his implacable opposition to non-denominational education, even when there was simply no alternative, he delayed the emergence of his people from their pitiful ignorance. The teachers, through their union, set the pace and in the decade 1868–78 did more for the betterment of their own status, the life-chances of the pupils entrusted to their care, and through them, the wider community, than had been achieved in the preceding half century.

Notes

ABBREVIATIONS

CD	*Catholic Directory*
CNEI	Commissioners of National Education in Ireland
CT	*Connaught Telegraph*
DDA	Dublin Diocesan Archives
DEP	*Dublin Evening Post*
HC	House of Commons
IAA	Irish Architectural Archives
ICM	Irish Church Missions
ITJ	*Irish Teachers' Journal*
MC	*Mayo Constitution*
MT	*Mayo Telegraph*
NA	National Archives
NLI	National Library of Ireland
TH	*Tuam Herald*

INTRODUCTION

1 Compiled from the *First report of the commissioners of public instruction in Ireland, province of Tuam, diocese of Tuam, class 1 rectories and vicarages*, pp 31d–79d, HC 1835 [45], xxxiii, 791–839.

2 *First report of the commissioners on public instruction*, pp 31d–46d, HC 1835 [45], xxxiii, 787–802.

3 Thomas Orde was Chief Secretary for Ireland 1784–7.

4 *Correspondence between Commissioners of Irish Education inquiry*, p. 4, H.C.1826–7 (518), xiii, 1140.

5 *Royal report, Royal commission on inquiry into education in Ireland*, appendix no. 3, p. 48, HC 1826–7 (510), xiii, 1046.

6 John MacHale, *The letters (1820–34) of the Most Rev Dr John MacHale* (Dublin, 1893), p. 492.

7 Hely Dutton, *Statistical and agricultural survey of the county of Galway* (Dublin, 1824), p. 259.

8 *Education in Ireland*, pp 1–2, HC 1831–31 (196), xxix, 757–8.

9 *Sixth report, CNEI*, 1839, (no. 2), quoting a letter from Bishop J. Doyle, diocese of Kildare and Leighlin to his clergy, HC 1840 (246), xxvii, 56.

ELEMENTARY EDUCATION IN THE ARCHDIOCESE OF TUAM, 1831–9

1 Monsignor E. D'Alton, *The history of the archdiocese of Tuam* (2 vols, Dublin, 1928), i, p. 370.

2 Bernard O'Reilly, *The life of John MacHale, archbishop of Tuam* (New York, 1890), i, p. 127.

3 O'Reilly, *MacHale*, i, p.128.

4 O'Reilly, *MacHale*, i. p. 91.

5 *Catholic Directory*, 1882, p. 238.

6 D'Alton, *Tuam*, i, p. 381.

7 D'Alton, *Tuam*, i, p. 377.

8 O'Reilly, *MacHale*, i, p. 91.

9 O'Reilly, *MacHale*, i, p. 91.

10 *Freeman's Journal*, 8 November 1881.

11 Peadar MacSuibhne, *Paul Cullen and his contemporaries with their letters from 1820–1982*, (5 vols Naas, 1961–77) i, p. 216.

12 D'Alton, *Tuam*, i, p. 340.

13 D'Alton, *Tuam*, i, p. 343.

14 Patrick Conlan, *Franciscan Ireland* (Mullingar, 1988), p. 94.

15 D'Alton, *Tuam*, i, p. 385.

16 O'Reilly, *MacHale*, i, p. 243.

17 *CD* 1842, p. 317.

18 O'Reilly, *MacHale*, i, p. 196.

19 O'Reilly, *MacHale*, ii, p. 13.

20 *Sixth report, CNEI 1830*, HC 1840 (246), xxvii, 56.

21 D'Arcy Sirr, *A memoir of the honourable and most reverend Power Le Poer Trench* (Dublin, 1845), p. 699.

22 *Stanley to Leinster*, p. 3, HC 1831–32 (196), xxix, 759.

23 *Second report CNEI*, 1834–5, HC 1835 (300), xxxv, 40.

24 *Second report CNEI*, 1834–, HC 1835 (300), xxxv, 40

25 *First report on conditions of poorer classes in Ireland,* supplement to appendix B, HC 1835 (368), xxxii, pt ii, 699.

26 *Evidence taken before her majesty's commissioners to inquire into the state of law and practice in respect to the occupation of land in Ireland,* witness 482, p. 446, HC 1845 (616), xx, 452.

27 James H. Tuke, *A visit to Connaught* (London, 1847), p. 5.

28 Tuke, *visit,* p. 10.

29 *Times,* 5 November 1847.

30 William P. Coyne, *Ireland, industrial and agriculture* (Dublin, 1901), p. 154. In 1899 the Congested Districts Board purchased 80,000 acres of the Dillon estate in County Mayo for £290,000, for division among its 4,200 tenants.

31 *Mayo Telegraph,* 28 September 1836.

32 Mr and Mrs S.C. Hall, *Handbooks for Ireland: the west and Connemara* (Dublin, 1853), p. 93.

33 *Fourth report, CNEI,* p. 3, HC 1837–8 (110), xxviii, 46.

34 NA, ED 1/33 f.54.

35 John Bernard Burke, *A genealogical and heraldic dictionary of the peerage and baronetages of the British empire* (London, 1853), p. 196.

36 Irish Church Missions, minute book 2, no. 552 (11), June 1851.

37 *First report of the commissioners on public instruction,* pp 34d–35d , HC 1835 (45), xxxiii, 792–3.

38 *First report of the commissioners on public instruction,* pp 34d–35d , HC 1835 (45), xxxiii, 792–3

39 Sirr, *Trench,* p. 699.

40 *Connaught Telegraph,* 9 June 1847.

41 *Tuam Herald,* 27 December 1851.

42 Donald Harmon Akenson, *The Irish experiment – the national system of education in nineteenth century Ireland* (London, 1970), pp 198–9.

43 Rev A. Dallas, *Story of the Irish Church Missions* (London, 1867), pp 104–5.

44 *CD* 1836, p. 141.

45 *First report of the commissioners on public instruction,* p. 53d, HC 1835 (45), xxxiii, 813.

46 NA, ED 1/33 f. 26.

47 NA, ED 1/33 ff 20, 27.

48 NA, ED 1/33 ff 3, 4, 5, 8.

49 NA, ED 1/33 ff 41–8; 74; 83–7.

50 NA, ED 1/33 ff 28–9; NA, ED 1/61 f. 10.

51 NA, ED 1/33 f. 26.

52 *Second report, CNEI 1834–5,* pp 43–5, HC 1835 (300), xxxx, 77–9. .

53 Rev Henry M'Manus, *Sketches of the Irish highlands* (London, 1863), p. 161.

54 NA, ED 1/33 f. 24.

55 NA, ED 1/33 f. 18.

56 *Twenty-fifth report, CNEI 1858,* appendix B, p. 182, HC 1860 (2593–1), xxv, 222.

57 *DEP,* 1 January 1838, letter from MacHale to Lord John Russell.

58 *DEP,* 1 January 1838, MacHale to Russell.

59 *DEP,* 1 January 1838, MacHale to Russell.

60 *DEP,* 17 May 1838, quoting Lord John Russell

61 Compiled from first to ninth report, CNEI 1834–42.

62 Jacqueline O'Brien and Desmond Guinness, *Dublin, a grand tour* (London,1994), p. 91.

63 NLI, MS 5529, CNEI, minutes of board meeting, 1 October 1834, vol A, p. 233.

64 Clerks were paid between £90–£120 p.a.; James Hill, hall porter £30 p.a.

65 *First report of the commissioners on public instruction,* p. 56d, HC 1835 (45), xxxiii, 816.

66 DDA, minutes of bishops' meeting 23 January 1839.

STRANGERS CAME TO TEACH
THEM THEIR WAYS

1 G. Kitson Clark, *The making of Victorian England* (London, 1962), p. 20.

2 *CD* 1839, p. 258.

3 *DEP,* 2 April 1840.

4 *CD* 1839, p. 258.

5 *CD* 1840, p. 307

6 *CD*1842, p. 317.

7 *CD*1842, p. 317.

8 *IAA,* Gal. Tuam, Presentation convent

9 *CD* 1843, 2 April 1840.

10 *Nation,* 18 February 1841.

11 Archbishop Murray favoured the National Schools system; he was a commissioner of national education in Ireland, 1831–51.
12 MacSuibhne, *Cullen,* i, p. 235.
13 MacSuibhne, *Cullen,* i, pp 231–5.
14 MacSuibhne, *Cullen,* i, p. 235.
15 *CD* 1843, p. 317.
16 *CD* 1843, p. 317.
17 *CD* 1854, p. 328.
18 *CD*1839, p. 258.
19 *CD* 1840, p. 307.
20 DDA, minutes of bishops' meeting, 11 November 1841.
21 DDA, Hamilton letters 36/5: 18 no. 7.
22 *CT*, 30 March 1842.
23 *CD* 1854, p. 328.
24 *CD* 1854, p. 333.
25 Gibbons was Professor of Humanities at Maynooth College, 1815–24.
26 NA, ED 1/33 f. 94.
27 NA, ED 1/33 f. 114.
28 NA, ED 1/61 ff 23–5; 58–9; 63.
29 NA, ED 1/33 1/61 f. 30.
30 NA, ED 1/33 f. 94.
31 NA, ED 1/33 f. 91.
32 NA, ED 1/33 f. 54.
33 NA, ED 1/33 ff 91–3.
34 NA, ED 1/33 f. 88.
35 *MT*, 28 September 1836.
36 NA, ED 1/33 1/61 ff 101, 103.
37 NA, ED 1/33 f. 66.
38 NA, ED 1/33 ff 67, 71, 73, 78, 50, 56, 4, 27.
39 NA, ED 1/33 f. 69.
40 *Census of Ireland 1891*, pt 1 vol iv, table xxxii, HC 1892 [C. 6685], xciii.
41 NA, ED1/61 f. 44.
42 *CT*, 6 July 1842.
43 NA ED 1/61 f. 48.
44 Sr Mary Pius O'Farrell, *Nano Nagle: woman of the Gospel* (Cork, 1991), p. 259.
45 John P. Harrington (ed.) *The English traveller in Ireland* (Dublin, 1991), p. 259.
46 *CD* 1840, p. 307.
47 *CD* 1842, p. 317.
48 *CD* 1843, p. 317.
49 *Roscommon Journal*, 8 August, 1846.
50 NA, Distress Papers 5166, 15 September 1846.
51 NA, Distress Papers 5179, 17 September 1846.
52 *CT*, 21 December 1846.
53 NA, CSORP 3/2/21/24, 16 September 1846.
54 *CD* 1849, p. 379.
55 D'Alton, *Tuam*, ii, p. 271.
56 *TH*, 11 May 1847.
57 *CD* 1849, p. 378.
58 *Galway Packet*, 24 April 1852.
59 *CD* 1853, p. 315.
60 ICM, minute book 2, no. 19 (10), June 1851.
61 Mrs A.R.C. Dallas, *Incidents in the life of the Rev ARC Dallas* (London, 1871), p. 335.
62 ICM, minute book 2, no. 19 (10), June 1851.
63 *TH*, 20 February 1847.
64 Mrs A.R.C. Dallas, *Rev Dallas*, p. 336.
65 Rev Alexander Dallas, *Story of the Irish Church Missions* (London, 1867), p. 32.
66 ICM, minute book 1, no. 148, 8 November 1849.
67 ICM, minute book 2, no. 19 (ii), June 1851.
68 *Galway Mercury*, 6 December 1851.
69 ICM, minute book 2, no. 7, June 1851.
70 Irish Church Mission schools were established in the Clifden area at Bundorragh, Salruck, Tully, Renvyle, Lettermore, Letterfrack, Cleggan, Aughris, Claddaghduff, Omey, Glan, Moyard, Ballyconree, Barnahalia, Barratrough, Fakerragh, Turbot Island, Derrygimla, Ballynahinch, Ballinaboy, Toomebeola, Bunowenbeg, Aillebrack, Duholla, Roundstone, Murvey and Moyrus.
71 ICM, minute book 5, no. 930, June 1852.
72 ICM, minute book 5, no. 1031–5, October 1852.
73 ICM, minute book 2, no. 576, 25 July 1851.
74 Alexander Dallas, *Story of the Irish Church Mission continued to the year 1869* (London, 1875), p. 190.
75 Patrick J. Corish (ed.), 'Irish College, Rome: Kirby papers' in *Archivium Hibernicum*, xxxi, (1973), p.55.
76 *Galway Mercury*, 5 January 1850.
77 NA, ED 1/33 ff 62; 64–70.
78 Corish, 'Irish College, Rome', p. 55.
79 Liam Ua Chadhain, *Venerable Archdeacon Kavanagh* (Knock, 1953).
80 *The Irish Builder*, v, no. 44, 15 October 1861, p. 264.
81 *CD* 1861 p. 222.
82 *The Irish Builder*, iii, no. 44, 15 October 1861, p. 264.
83 *IAA*, Gal Clifden, Convent of Mercy.
84 *The Irish Builder*, iii, no. 44, 15 October 1861, p. 264.

85 *CD* 1854, p.333.
86 NA, ED 1/35 f.6.
87 *The Irish Builder*, iii, no. 44, 15 October 1861, p. 264.
88 IAA, May, Ballinrobe, Convent of Mercy.
89 *Galway Packet*, 19 May 1852.

TEACHER DEVELOPMENT AND LOCAL LEADERSHIP

1 *Twenty-second report, CNEI*, 1855, appendix D, p. 44, H.C. 1856 (2142–1), xxvii, 52.
2 *Forty-fifth report, CNEI,* 1878, appendix B, p. 77, HC 1878–79 [C.2031–1], xxiv, 633.
3 *Twenty-second report, CNEI*, 1855, appendix D, p.66, HC 1856 [2142–1], xxvii, 74.
4 *Sixteenth report, CNEI,* 1849, p. 9, HC 1850 [1231], xxv, 220.
5 *Twenty-eighth report, CNEI*, 1861, appendix C, p. 291, H.C. 1862 [3026–1], xx, 539.
6 *Twenty-ninth report, CNEI*, 1862, appendix D, p. 170, H.C. 1862 [3235–1], xvii, 356.
7 *Twenty-ninth report, CNEI*, 1862, appendix D, p. 243, H.C. 1862 [3235–1], xvii, 423
8 *Twenty-ninth report, CNEI*, 1862, appendix D, p. 245, H.C. 1862 [3235–1], xvii, 425.
9 NA, ED 2/112 f.10.
10 *Mayo Constitution*, 12 February 1856
11 *Twenty-ninth report, CNEI*, 1862, appendix D, p.243, H.C. 1863 [3235–1], xvii, 423.
12 *Return of names of schools in connection with the Board of National Education in Ireland 1864, Pt iv, Province of Connaught*, pp 5–95, H.C. 1864 [481–111], xlvii, 667–757.
13 *Papers relating to convent schools, Ireland*, p. 47, H.C. 1864 (179), xlvi, 47.
14 *Twenty-ninth report, CNEI, 1862*, appendix D, p.243 H.C. 1863 [3235–1], xvii, 423.
15 *Papers relating to national education, Ireland*, p. 4, no. 3, H.C. 1867 (473), iv, 734.
16 *Royal commission on nature and extent of instruction by institutions in Ireland for elementary or primary education, and working of system of national education*, H.C. 1870 [C.6], xxviii, pt 1.1.
17 University of Toronto, *Dictionary of Canadian Biography* (Toronto, 1982), p. 535.
18 *Irish Teachers' Journal*, October 1868.
19 *ITJ*, each edition.
20 *ITJ*, 1 January 1868.
21 *ITJ*, 1 January 1868.
22 *ITJ*, 15 August 1874.
23 *ITJ*, 1 October 1868.
24 *Twenty-eighth report, CNEI*, 1861, appendix C, p. 292, H.C. 1862 [3026–1], xx, 540.
25 *Sixteenth report, CNEI*, 1849, p. 6, H.C. 1850 [1231][1231–11], xxv, 126.
26 NA, ED 2/129 f. 31.
27 *Thirty-first report, CNEI*, 1864, appendix D, p. 246 H.C. 1865[3496–1], xxxi, 286.
28 *ITJ*, 5 February 1876.
29 *ITJ*, 19 February 1876.
30 *Sixteenth report, CNEI*, 1849, p. 7, H.C. 1850 [1231][1231–11], xxv, 127.
31 *ITJ*, 5 October 1878.
32 *ITJ*, 5 October 1878.
33 *Forty-fifth report, CNEI*, 1878, appendix B, p. 77, H.C.1878–79, [C.2031], xxix, 633.
34 *ITJ*, 18 September 1876.
35 *ITJ*, 1 March 1868.
36 *ITJ*, 1 September 1868.
37 *Fifty-first report, CNEI*, 1884, appendix C, p. 224–5, H.C. 1884–5 [C.4458–1], xxiv, 540–1.
38 *Correspondence relative to national schools, Ireland, (Teaching of Irish)*, no. 1, p. 3, H.C. 1884 (81), lxi, 617.
39 NA, ED 1/36 f. 98.
40 *Forty-eighth report, CNEI*, 1881, appendix B, p. 55, H.C.1881, [C.3243], xxiv, 131.
41 NA, ED 1/78 f. 10.
42 NA, ED 1/102 f. 164.
43 Donald Harman Akenson, *The Irish Diaspora* (Toronto, 1996), p. 257.
44 Liam Ua Cadhain, *Cavanagh*, pp 81, 85
45 *Tuam News*, 24 March 1882, quoting a letter dated 4 February 1882 from Thomas MacHale, the archbishop's nephew and executor.
46 Michael J. O'Brien, *A hidden phase of American history* (Baltimore, 1973), p. 504.
47 *MC*, 13 August 1870.
48 *MC*, 27 August 1870.

Maynooth Research Guides for Irish Local History

IN THIS SERIES

Maynooth Studies in Irish Local History

IN THIS SERIES

Maynooth Studies in Irish Local History (cont.)